WELCOME TO FOUR WAY:
The Town That Time Forgot

A Comedy in Two Acts
by
KENT R. BROWN

Dramatic Publishing
Woodstock, Illinois • London, England • Melbourne, Australia

*** NOTICE ***

The amateur and stock acting rights to this work are controlled exclusively by THE DRAMATIC PUBLISHING COMPANY without whose permission in writing no performance of it may be given. Royalty fees are given in our current catalogue and are subject to change without notice. Royalty must be paid every time a play is performed whether or not it is presented for profit and whether or not admission is charged. A play is performed anytime it is acted before an audience. All inquiries concerning amateur and stock rights should be addressed to:

DRAMATIC PUBLISHING
P. O. Box 129, Woodstock, Illinois 60098.

COPYRIGHT LAW GIVES THE AUTHOR OR THE AUTHOR'S AGENT THE EXCLUSIVE RIGHT TO MAKE COPIES. This law provides authors with a fair return for their creative efforts. Authors earn their living from the royalties they receive from book sales and from the performance of their work. Conscientious observance of copyright law is not only ethical, it encourages authors to continue their creative work. This work is fully protected by copyright. No alterations, deletions or substitutions may be made in the work without the prior written consent of the publisher. No part of this work may be reproduced or transmitted in any form or by any means, electronic or mechanical, including photocopy, recording, videotape, film, or any information storage and retrieval system, without permission in writing from the publisher. It may not be performed either by professionals or amateurs without payment of royalty. All rights, including but not limited to the professional, motion picture, radio, television, videotape, foreign language, tabloid, recitation, lecturing, publication, and reading are reserved. *On all programs this notice should appear:*

"Produced by special arrangement with
THE DRAMATIC PUBLISHING COMPANY of Woodstock, Illinois"

©MCMXCIII by
KENT R. BROWN

Printed in the United States of America
All Rights Reserved
(WELCOME TO FOUR WAY: The Town That Time Forgot)

Cover design by Susan Carle

ISBN 0-87129-303-X

WELCOME TO FOUR WAY:
The Town That Time Forgot

A Comedy in Two Acts
For Seven Men and Six Women

CHARACTERS

MAURICE DARCY . . . . a man in his later years
CHERYL MAE DOBBINS . . . . 19 years of age, an athlete
"VULGAR" VICTOR BOSCO . in his 40s, a Vietnam veteran
STANLEY FRANK . . late 40s, self-appointed town historian
COLLEEN KIMBEL .late 30s, divorced
HARRIET MUELLER . . . . in her late 40s, runs a small store
JACKSON PURDY . . . . in his early 40s,
           self-appointed head of Chamber of Commerce
DARYL SWEETWOOD . . . . in his early 20s,
               works for the highway department
BOBBY JAMES DOBBINS . . . . 18 years of age,
                         Cheryl Mae's brother
GEORGIA SWEENEY . . . . in her upper years
HAROLD SWEENEY . . . . her husband
AMY LYNN PURDY . . . . in her 30s, Jackson's wife
LUCINDA HARRIS . . . late 20s, hitchhiking across America

TIME:

The present. Mid-August.

ACT ONE   Morning before Noon
ACT TWO   Near Sunset

PLACE:

We are in the town of Four Way, a small rural community where two roads met over a century ago. A large tree dominates the setting. A few dead branches suggest the dryness of the environment. An old pay telephone, and a sign proclaiming WELCOME TO FOUR WAY, are attached to the tree. A circular wooden bench has been constructed around the base of the tree. In the vicinity are a dilapidated car seat, several old chairs, a wooden crate or two, and some wood shavings. This is where people meet throughout the day to visit, play cards, whittle and tell stories, some of which are true.

WELCOME TO FOUR WAY: The Town That Time Forgot
made its world premiere at Northern Kentucky University's
Department of Theatre Y.E.S. Festival on April 15, 1993,
with the following cast:

Maurice Darcy . . . . *Scott Thrasher*
Cheryl Mae Dobbins . . . . *Carlie Schulenberg*
"Vulgar" Victor Bosco . . . . *Neil David Seibel*
Stanley Frank . . . . *Fred Caldwell*
Colleen Kimbel . . . . *Jami Menkhaus*
Harriet Mueller . . . . *Kim Wade*
Jackson Purdy . . . . *Watson Kenneth Brown*
Bobby James Dobbins . . . . *Kristian Allen*
Amy Lynn Purdy . . . . *Michelle Bardo*
Georgia Sweeney . . . . *Michele McLean*
Harold Sweeney . . . . *Huey Scott Pergrem*
Daryl Sweetwood . . . . *Marcus Schulte*
Lucinda Harris . . . . *Spring Starr Pillow*

Directed by . . . . *Sandra Forman*
Scenic Designer . . . . *Ronald A. Shaw*
Costume Designer . . . . *Gretchen H. Sears*
Lighting Designer & Technical Director . . *Jeffrey M. Gress*
Sound Designer . . . . *Gary W. Poole*
Stage Manager . . . . *Claudia Cartolano*

ACT ONE

AT THE CURTAIN: *MAURICE DARCY stands looking out over the audience. He is well dressed in a dark suit and white spats. He carries an umbrella as well as a thermos and small cooler. After surveying the "landscape," he moves to the tree bench where he takes out a large red handkerchief, places it on the bench, and seats himself upon it. He pours a cup of coffee, smiles, extends his arm in a toast to no one we can see.*

MAURICE. Good morning, Margaret. Did you sleep well? Do you sleep at all, I wonder. *(Beat.)* Going to be a scorcher. *(He takes a sip of coffee then closes his eyes. A basketball rolls through the setting and into the wings. MAURICE glances at the ball and then closes his eyes once again. The effect is almost surreal.)*

(A moment later CHERYL MAE DOBBINS enters, sees MAURICE with his eyes closed, and quietly begins to cross the stage.)

MAURICE. Good morning, Cheryl Mae.

CHERYL MAE. Good morning, Mr. Darcy. Didn't mean to disturb you.

MAURICE. You weren't.

CHERYL MAE. Looked like you were praying.

MAURICE. Your basketball went that way, I think. Rolled right by.

CHERYL MAE. Yes, sir. Hit off my foot.

MAURICE. You're supposed to dribble basketballs, aren't you?

CHERYL MAE. Didn't sleep much last night.

MAURICE. When we played the game we'd take it to the center of the court after we made a basket and jump it up and do it all again.

CHERYL MAE. Yes, sir.

MAURICE. Game's changed a lot since then, hasn't it? Fast break, slam dunk, High Five, lots of "x's" and "o's." In my day the tall kid was in the center. Everybody else stood around on the outside.

CHERYL MAE. Yes, sir.

MAURICE. Scored nine points…you'd get the keys to the city.

CHERYL MAE. Yes, sir.

MAURICE. You and Bobby James safe enough?

CHERYL MAE. We're doing fine. Thank you.

MAURICE. It's going to be a hot one.

CHERYL MAE. Yesterday it was 97 degrees at 9:00 a.m.

MAURICE. Is that right?

CHERYL MAE. Radio said so.

MAURICE. Must be true then. (*CHERYL MAE exits after the basketball.*) Well, Margaret, it's going to be another wonderful day in Four Way. (*Beat.*) Hope you slept well.

(*VICTOR BOSCO enters. VICTOR is a slightly disoriented Vietnam veteran who wears combat pants and a sleeveless fatigue shirt. He is dribbling CHERYL MAE's basketball. CHERYL MAE is in close pursuit.*)

VICTOR *(dribbling around the tree).* Only eight seconds to go. Game's all tied up. And "Vulgar" Victor moves it down the court for the Harrison Mustangs. Doesn't look good for the Four Way Bulldogs. But wait…out of nowhere comes Cheryl Mae Dobbins. *(CHERYL MAE begins to defend against VICTOR. They both play out the action.)* A contest of titanic tension, folks. The crowd's cheering. Maurice! *(MAURICE makes cheering sounds.)* Cheryl Mae steals the ball. There she goes! Down the court! Three… two…one! And it's up…up…*(VICTOR makes a circle by extending his arms as CHERYL MAE shoots the ball through the "hoop.")* The Bulldogs win!

MAURICE. Bravo, bravo. Well done, Cheryl Mae!

VICTOR. Cheryl Mae Dobbins does it again. *(Beat.)* Shoulda made All Conference, Cheryl Mae. They screwed ya over.

CHERYL MAE. Maybe next year, Victor.

VICTOR. You keep shootin' now.

CHERYL MAE. I am. An hour a day.

VICTOR. It's all in the wrist, you hear me? Follow through.

CHERYL MAE. Thanks. I'll remember.

VICTOR *(fixating on MAURICE's spats).* Hey, Maurice! What are you wearing on your feet? Cheryl Mae, get a load of those.

MAURICE. They're called spats.

VICTOR. Oh, yeah. Spats. My granddaddy used to wear those. Even wore 'em in the box when they put him under.

MAURICE. No need to be offensive.

VICTOR. I liked my granddaddy, Maurice. Heck of a lot.

MAURICE. I feel better already. Thank you, Victor.

VICTOR *(a bit erratic).* You bet! My pleasure. It's gonna be hot today. Better hide and rest. *(VICTOR sits down in the shade and holds the basketball tightly to his chest as if holding a fallen comrade. MAURICE and CHERYL MAE are unsurprised by VICTOR's behavior.)* Bam! Bam! Bam! You're here...

MAURICE *(to VICTOR).* Have you had your breakfast this morning?

VICTOR. Then you're gone. Just like that! Up! Then down.

MAURICE. Victor?

VICTOR. I hear ya.

MAURICE. Give the ball back to Cheryl Mae.

CHERYL MAE. That's all right, Mr. Darcy.

MAURICE. You're not in the jungle anymore, Victor. You can relax. You're part of civilization now.

VICTOR. Right here in Four Way?

MAURICE. That's correct. Right here in Four Way. *(VICTOR rolls the basketball toward CHERYL MAE.)*

CHERYL MAE. Thank you, Victor. I brought this for the garage sale.

VICTOR. You're up...then you're down.

MAURICE. Cheryl Mae, do me a favor and drop in at the Oasis for me, will you?

VICTOR *(energized).* It's donut time! Front and center!

MAURICE. We'll need...

VICTOR. Ten glazed, five sugar, three strawberry, three lemon, a dozen chocolate with those little sprinkle things on top, and a bran muffin for old Maurice here. State of the art breakfast chow for our elderly comrade.

MAURICE. How considerate.

VICTOR. Gotta take care of your roughage, Maurice.

MAURICE. I'll take care of my own roughage, but thank you for the thought.

CHERYL MAE. I can help, Mr. Darcy. I've got money.

MAURICE *(reaching into his wallet).* That's okay, Cheryl Mae, but my social security check arrived yesterday.

VICTOR. Don't let him work you like that, Cheryl Mae. He's rollin' in shit.

MAURICE. Your descriptive powers overwhelm me, Victor.

(STANLEY FRANK enters quickly, carrying a variety of journals, papers, and old photographs. He is distinguished by an intriguing blend of shyness and unbounded enthusiasm.)

STANLEY. I set the...alarm. I know I did. Slept right through it. What was I thinking!! Couldn't decide about what to bring today. Are they here yet? *(STANLEY hands his items to CHERYL MAE.)* Please hold these. I thought they would give a fascinating...account of...when it's opened the next time. How the town began...I mean. Who we were...and where we've been...*(Looking offstage.)* Oh, dear...is that the machine there? Lovely morning isn't it. Hello, everyone...happy birthday...big day...important day! *(STANLEY exits in a flurry.)*

MAURICE. Stanley seems in good spirits.

VICTOR. He's wacky, ever notice that, Maurice? Kinda strange. Not like you and me.

MAURICE. We're all distinctive, Victor.

CHERYL MAE *(looking offstage)*. They've arrived. I think they're here.

MAURICE. Add in a few extra donuts for the workers, Cheryl Mae.

VICTOR *(coaxing MAURICE)*. It's gonna be a scorcher, Maurice.

MAURICE. And some cold pop.

VICTOR. My man!

MAURICE *(softly to CHERYL MAE)*. And some orange juice for Victor. And tell Harriet to come when she can.

CHERYL MAE. Yes, sir. I'll be right back. *(CHERYL MAE exits. Sounds of heavy machinery digging up concrete and changing gears can be heard intermittently. MAURICE pours himself another cup of coffee from his thermos, and then inserts a cigarette into his cigarette holder. He lights his cigarette and crosses his legs. All of this is a ritual he's performed thousands of times before. VICTOR withdraws a pocket knife and begins to whittle on a piece of wood.)*

VICTOR. It's gettin' hotter every year, Maurice. One of these days the sky will burn away and the planets will fall...and great demons from beneath the earth will rise above us all.

MAURICE. It's not the prettiest of options, but you're not alone in your predictions, Victor.

VICTOR. Used to drive a dozer in the other world so I know what it's like to see planets fall from the sky. Ever tell you about the other world, Maurice?

MAURICE. Numerous times. But you go ahead.

VICTOR. It wasn't like real life.

MAURICE. So you've said.

VICTOR. We shouldn't be allowed to do those things.

MAURICE. I agree.

VICTOR *(with energy)*. I think I'm getting better, Maurice. Get up every morning and say to myself, "Get better, damn it!" Makes me feel better anyway. *(Beat.)* Do you think I'm getting any better?

MAURICE. You're doing quite well, Victor.

VICTOR. I think about killing myself sometimes.

MAURICE. Most of us have given it a thought now and then. Nothing unusual. Don't let it get you down.

VICTOR *(quickly changing tempo)*. I didn't know what to bring for the next century, did you? "A piece of my life," Stanley said. Hell, who'd know what to do with it? I don't.

Damn progress'll kill you every time. (*Beat.*) What's it like when nothin's the same anymore?

MAURICE. You ask hard questions, Victor. Those are the best kind. I've always liked that about you. The ones no one can answer.

(*COLLEEN KIMBEL enters. She is six months pregnant.*)

COLLEEN. Hello, Maurice.

MAURICE. Good morning, Colleen. Are you all set? Anything I can do?

COLLEEN. I don't know if I'm all set, Maurice. But today's the day.

VICTOR. Colleen!

COLLEEN. Hello, Victor.

VICTOR. My heart! My heart!

COLLEEN (*has heard VICTOR's sentiments frequently*). Thank you, Victor. That's generous of you.

VICTOR (*referring to COLLEEN's pregnancy.*) Whose is it, Colleen?

COLLEEN. Not now, Victor.

VICTOR. You can tell me. Whisper in my ear. I won't tell a soul.

COLLEEN. You're being vulgar, Victor.

VICTOR. You say the nicest things, Colleen.

COLLEEN (*to MAURICE*). The house closes at two o'clock this afternoon. Should be able to get a few hundred miles behind me...get a room...watch CNN...have a good cry. I'll do fine.

VICTOR. Take me with you.

COLLEEN. Not this time, Victor.

MAURICE. We'll miss you, Colleen.

COLLEEN (*kisses MAURICE on the forehead*). You're sweet, Maurice. Margaret was a very lucky woman.

VICTOR. My forehead's over this way, Colleen. (*COLLEEN pauses a moment and then kisses VICTOR on the forehead.*) Did you see that Maurice? She kissed me! (*To COLLEEN.*) I got other places on my body if you're really interested.

(*CHERYL MAE enters with several sacks of donuts, coffee, and cokes.*)

CHERYL MAE. Ten glazed, five sugar, three strawberry, three lemon and a dozen chocolate with those little...

VICTOR. Sprinkle things!

CHERYL MAE. Two muffins for you, Mr. Darcy, and six glazed for the highway workers. Orange juice and pop cans in this bag.

VICTOR (*finds the orange juice and gulps it down quickly*). I'm kind of a problem at times. I'm sorry.

CHERYL MAE. That's okay.

VICTOR. Tastes good. Thanks.

COLLEEN (*helping CHERYL MAE with the sacks*). Here, let me help you with these.

CHERYL MAE (*to MAURICE*). Here's the change.

MAURICE. You keep it. Put it in your piggy bank. It's a special day.

CHERYL MAE (*giving all the change to MAURICE*). Bobby's got the route, Mr. Darcy, and the second shift at the plant. And I've got a new job at Babcock's. But thank you just the same.

VICTOR. Doin' what?

CHERYL MAE. The books and some typing.

VICTOR. You be sure the door's open, you here?

COLLEEN. Victor, people have to learn about people for themselves.

VICTOR *(to CHERYL MAE)*. You hear me? Tell him to keep his hands on the table and his sausage in the freezer.

MAURICE. I think Cheryl Mae gets the general idea.

CHERYL MAE. I'll be okay. Thanks, Victor.

VICTOR. Your father woulda told ya the same thing. The moment Babcock's hands start rising up off the table top... just let me know...and I'll waste him.

COLLEEN. Nice offer, Victor.

VICTOR. It's just the kinda guy I am, Colleen.

COLLEEN. You're a hell of a friend, Victor, I'll say that for you.

(STANLEY enters carrying a rather large stone. It has been uncovered during the "off stage" digging. He displays it with enthusiasm.)

STANLEY. Look...see? Look! I found it. Just looked down and there it was. They stopped digging so I could get it out. See?

VICTOR. Where? See what?

STANLEY. Right here! Don't you see?

VICTOR *(looking closely at the rock)*. It's a rock. So what? I've seen lots of rocks, Stanley. I've been around.

STANLEY. Tracks...history...right here!

VICTOR. Oh, yeah! Looks like a bug or a fish-something or other. A rib cage maybe. Hey, this is something.

STANLEY *(showing it to EVERYONE)*. Bones, I think. Absolutely amazing. Under the ocean...right where we are now...for thousands of years. With all that...pressure...and all that...decay...deep in the mud...and the pressure forming around it year after year after year...until...

VICTOR. Yeah, I got it! Right! He's just mindin' his own business...out for a swim maybe or sittin' underneath a tree...and all that pressure just squeezed down around that poor sucker and zap! Instant fossil. Just like that! Musta really surprised him.

MAURICE. I think it takes a little longer than that, Victor.

VICTOR. Not in my story it doesn't.

COLLEEN *(sincerely)*. I didn't know Four Way was under the ocean a long time ago.

STANLEY *(captivated by COLLEEN)*. Yes, we were. I mean...the earth...the land was.

COLLEEN. It's all very fascinating, Stanley. I'll miss you.

STANLEY. Thank you. *(Beat.)* You look...ah...very...

VICTOR *(beat)*. Sweet. Tell her she looks sweet.

STANLEY *(beat)*. Nice. You look very nice today. I'm sorry you're leaving.

COLLEEN. Thank you, Stanley.

VICTOR. Ask her for a kiss on your forehead.

STANLEY. I have to go. *(STANLEY suddenly exits, carrying the rock with him.)*

VICTOR. I'm doing better than Stanley is, Maurice, don't you think?

MAURICE. He's busy today, Victor. Has his mind on several things.

VICTOR *(begins to move in an agitated manner)*. It's the heat. Why's all the bad stuff happen in the heat? All that pressure.

CHERYL MAE. Mr. Darcy?

VICTOR. Tall kid...six foot, four inches...

COLLEEN. Victor?

VICTOR. Jimmy Loon...from Louisiana.

MAURICE. Victor?

COLLEEN. How 'bout one of these chocolate donuts you like so much with the sprinkle things...

VICTOR. Two teeth missing right in front. Looked like a crooked fence without a gate. You hearin' me, troopers?

MAURICE. We hear you, Victor.

VICTOR. Supposed to be a short run. In and out. Back in time for Johnny Carson. Still had his hair up. Jimmy used to roll his hair up. In a bun. And prance around the NCO club on his off-duty time. Had a chickie searching high and low for a pair of big red heels. Size thirteen! Just gave up and had a pair handmade for him. Cost her a month on her back, but she loved him. Sally Louise. That was the name of his girlfriend in Shreveport. He missed her a lot. So he dressed up like her so he wouldn't forget her in all the shit he had to deal with. Jimmy's name was Jimmy. You tracking all this? *(VICTOR's pocket knife is still in his hand. No one is particularly anxious about his behavior, but they're playing it safe. VICTOR moves low to the ground as if on night patrol.)*

CHERYL MAE. Should we call somebody?

(STANLEY enters carrying another rock.)

STANLEY. Look! Another one. See? Two in the same... *(STANLEY sees VICTOR and freezes.)*

VICTOR *(lowering his left arm to his side and squatting down on his haunches).* So, he gives us the "get down" and we get down. Even the bugs was silent...like they was holding their breath...like they knew what was going down. "Hey, sweet thing," he says, talkin' to the darkness, "you got something for me tonight?"

COLLEEN. Where's Harriet?

CHERYL MAE. She said she'd be right along.

MAURICE. I'd appreciate it, Victor, if you'd put down that knife.

VICTOR. Kept cocking his head and listening. He had the best pair of ears in the show. Big floppy things like a bat. Could hear a gnat fart at fifty paces.

CHERYL MAE. You can come over for dinner tonight, Victor, and shoot some hoops.

(HARRIET MUELLER enters quietly. She is crusty woman and rather blunt.)

VICTOR. Then Jimmy peeks his head up a little to see what he could see...

HARRIET *(adopts a martial arts posture).* And standing ten feet away was his worst nightmare. Lookee here, G.I., I've come to take you away! Chop...chop! *(VICTOR takes a similar stance and makes strange chanting sounds.)*

MAURICE. Hello, Harriet, You're looking well this morning.

HARRIET. Not now, Maurice. I've got my hands full. *(VICTOR and HARRIET begin circling each other. Each will execute several martial arts moves without making direct contact. The pocket knife is still in VICTOR's hand.)* This is not the day to live it all again, Victor. I need you at the store. Mrs. Randall wants some help with one of the new barbecues. Her great-uncle is coming over and she wants to fire him up some of her famous ribs before he dies, but she is in that walker of hers, Victor, and she can't assemble the damn thing by herself. Can barely open the box. That's where you come in, commando. She wants you to put it together. It's another five dollars for us, big boy. And every little bit counts. So cut this crap and get squared away. You hear me? God's speaking, G.I.!

VICTOR *(snapping to attention).* I hear you, Sergeant Major!

HARRIET. Good. You keep listening, you hear?

VICTOR. Yo!

HARRIET *(warmly)*. You're safe now, sweetheart. No more war. It's over. Give me the knife. *(From offstage we hear the voice of JACKSON PURDY approaching.)*

JACKSON *(from off)*. Good morning, gentlemen. Have everything you need? Gonna be a real scorcher, yes sir! If you need anything…I mean absolutely anything…

(JACKSON enters rolling a cart from which are suspended several inflated balloons and a sign reading, "It's a Big Day for Four Way!" The cart carries a multi-gallon ice cooler with a sign hanging on it reading "Free Lemonade—2¢.")

JACKSON. Happy Birthday everyone! It's a lovely day for a…*(JACKSON stops suddenly when he sees VICTOR and HARRIET.)* Oh, damn.

COLLEEN. Keep your pants on Jackson. We're almost finished.

JACKSON. Not today. Any day but today. Everything's been…

HARRIET. The knife, Victor. It's okay. *(HARRIET extends her hand to VICTOR who gives her the knife.)* At ease, soldier. *(VICTOR moves into the "at ease" position but sways a bit. He is exhausted.)* You can breathe now, Stanley. The range is clear. Okay, Maurice, it's your turn.

MAURICE. Hello again, Harriet. You still look well this morning.

HARRIET. That's generous of you, Maurice. Considering.

JACKSON. Can we get on with the festivities now?

VICTOR. I don't think I'm getting better, Maurice.

MAURICE. It takes time, Victor. You're doing fine.

STANLEY. She disarmed him like Rambo. Just stared him down like...Rambo. *(VICTOR bursts into laughter. The tension has broken. VICTOR sits on the ground. HARRIET takes out a handkerchief and wipes off VICTOR's forehead.)*

JACKSON. Here, somebody, take these balloons and help me set up the lemonade stand, please. *(CHERYL MAE helps JACKSON with the balloons and the lemonade display. STANLEY will shortly begin making notes and occasionally take Polaroid snapshots of the balloons, the people, and the setting. COLLEEN seems aloof, unaware; MAURICE, HARRIET, VICTOR and CHERYL MAE take no notice. JACKSON is always looking for a "photo opportunity.")*

CHERYL MAE. Mr. Darcy bought donuts for everyone, Mr. Purdy. Would you like...

JACKSON. No time for donuts. The reporter from the *Times Record* will be here soon...and I want us to look...what's the word?

HARRIET. Festive?

JACKSON. Festive, yes. That's the perfect word. Thank you, Harriet.

HARRIET. Well, thank you, Jackson. I wouldn't know what festive was if it weren't for these gawdawful balloons bouncing around in the air.

JACKSON. It's not everyday we get a four-way stop sign smack dab in the middle of Four Way, Harriet. *(Beat.)* That's real clever, don't you think? A four-way stop sign in Four Way.

VICTOR. Can barely keep my guts in.

JACKSON. A sign of progress. Growth. Hope. A new future.

COLLEEN. You sound like a brochure, Jackson.

JACKSON. I finished it last night. They'll be ready next week.

VICTOR. A stop sign don't mean we're growin'. Means there are too many cars in the world. Ought to go back to covered wagons. They were big. Could see those suckers for miles. Didn't sneak up on ya outta the bushes the way cars do.

JACKSON. We'll have to widen the street here pretty soon, too.

HARRIET. How do you propose to widen the street, Jackson. Cut down the tree?

JACKSON. Of course. How else?

VICTOR (*beat*). What'd you say?

JACKSON. Can't hold back progress. It's coming over the hill.

VICTOR. There's no hill around here, Jackson.

MAURICE. I don't think that would be a good...

JACKSON. Limbs are dying. Look at it.

VICTOR. This is the Talking Tree, Jackson. Don't you hear us talkin' here?

JACKSON. This whole place is an eye sore, Victor. Look at it! Telephone hasn't worked in the whole time I've been here. Junk all around everywhere.

VICTOR. God calls us now and then, Jackson. You're just not around to hear it.

JACKSON. The wire's been cut!

VICTOR. God don't need no telephone wires, Jackson. You don't know crap.

JACKSON. Well, can't just do things the old way. Have to grow...expand.

HARRIET. Some things you don't change, Jackson. Stay around a while longer. Unpack your bags. You'll get the hang of it.

CHERYL MAE (*trying to lighten the tension*). Why are you charging two cents for free lemonade, Mr. Purdy?

JACKSON. It's a joke, Cheryl Mae.

HARRIET. That's a scream, Jackson. I can barely stay on my feet.

JACKSON. That's not the joke.

HARRIET. Silly me.

JACKSON. When I was a boy my dad made me a lemonade stand and I would set it up out in front of his grocery store. And on hot summer days I would sit outside and call out "Lemonade! Lemonade! Two cents a glass!"

VICTOR. Clever gimmick.

MAURICE. Victor, let him have his say.

JACKSON. And customers would stop for a glass and leave a few pennies in a plate. But, you can't buy anything for two cents today, so might as well give it away!

HARRIET. Is that it?

JACKSON. Yes!

COLLEEN. Worth waiting for if you ask me. *(STANLEY snaps a Polaroid of JACKSON standing next to the lemonade stand.)*

JACKSON. Thanks for helping, Cheryl Mae. Your father would be proud of you.

VICTOR *(moves quickly toward JACKSON who holds his ground)*. You never met her father you slimeball! How the hell would you know how he'd feel? The paint on your house ain't even dry yet!

HARRIET. Victor!

VICTOR. Stupid ass balloons everywhere. Hell, it's just another hot day in the middle of nowhere. And that's how we like it. Most of us anyway. 'Til you came along...started a Chamber of Commerce of one. Shit! Ain't been no commerce in thirty years...just people gettin' up and wonderin' what it's all about. So why don't you go back where you came from?

MAURICE. Moving too fast in hot weather tires a man out, Jackson. I think that's what Victor is saying. How about a sip of some cool lemonade?

(Another awkward pause and then DARYL SWEETWOOD enters. He is dressed in highway construction clothes.)

DARYL. Excuse me.

JACKSON *(extends his hand)*. Hi, there! My name's Jackson Purdy. I'm with the Chamber here. How do you do?

DARYL *(shaking JACKSON's hand)*. My name's Daryl Sweetwood.

JACKSON. What can I do for you, Mr. Sweetwood? Anything at all. Just name it.

DARYL. Is there a bathroom nearby?

VICTOR. I'd like to see you do that for the kid, Jackson.

COLLEEN. Up at the Oasis. Big green palm tree on the roof. Can't miss it. Only restaurant in town.

JACKSON *(to DARYL)*. Got everything you need? If not, just call it out. I'll bring it right up.

HARRIET. Give him some air, Jackson.

DARYL. I think we'll make it, sir. Thank you.

HARRIET. You came to put in the stop sign?

DARYL. Yes, ma'am. Sorry we're late. My partner and me never been here before.

VICTOR. Few people have. We're sort of out of the way.

DARYL. Sure is hot here.

MAURICE. Where you from, Daryl?

DARYL. Harrison.

CHERYL MAE. I've been to Harrison. They've got a Pizza Hut there.

DARYL. Yeah, I work there on the weekends now. Make a little extra money.

JACKSON. That's nothing. Four Way's going to have a Taco Bell, a Holiday Inn, a Pizza Palace…and a…

DARYL. Yes, sir. Ah, where's that Oasis place you said?

VICTOR *(pointing)*. No problem. You go down this way 'til you hit…

CHERYL MAE. I'm going that way. I'll show you.

DARYL. Thank you.

VICTOR. It's not like we got a thousand miles of sidewalk in this town, Cheryl Mae. *(DARYL and CHERYL MAE begin to exit.)*

CHERYL MAE. I'm going to check on Bobby James. Said he'd meet me at the bank.

DARYL *(to CHERYL MAE)*. Didn't you play for the Bulldogs?

CHERYL MAE. Yeah, sometimes.

DARYL. My kid brother's gettin' pretty good, practices every…*(He and CHERYL MAE exit.)*

VICTOR *(starting to follow DARYL and CHERYL MAE)*. I better chaperone this thing, Harriet. Bring along some donuts maybe.

HARRIET. Quit stalling, Victor. Mrs. Randall won't live forever. I'll be there in a minute. And take your medicine. It's in the…

VICTOR. All right, but I'm tellin' ya, this is my last day in Four Way. I've had enough excitement around here to last me a lifetime! My endorphines are zinging. No more. *Kaput!* You hear me, Harriet?

HARRIET. Everyday, Victor.

VICTOR. Victor was here! Don't you ever forget that. *(He exits by executing a series of martial arts moves.)*

COLLEEN. Is he taking his medicine?

HARRIET. Says he is. Barely eats what I fix for him at the farm. Has nightmares. Wakes up in the middle of the night crying sometimes.

COLLEEN. Hasn't come into the Oasis in weeks.

HARRIET. Maybe it's the heat. Need some rain!

JACKSON *(puttering around the stand)*. The man's unstable. He needs assistance. He should be...

HARRIET *(with anger)*. It's none of your damn business, Jackson. He has assistance. He has me. Just play with your lemons.

JACKSON *(beat)*. Amy Lynn will be here in a minute. Anybody come along for some lemonade, tell 'em it's free. The two cents was a joke. I told you that, didn't I? I got a lot more where that came from.

HARRIET. I bet.

JACKSON *(beat)*. I'm sorry, Harriet. That was rude of me. *(He exits.)*

STANLEY. Awful things must have...happened to Victor. Awful. History tries...to...be...better...but we keep... doing...awful things.

MAURICE *(pulling a bottle of champagne out of his small cooler, along with several plastic champagne glasses)*. Well, cheer up, everyone. A special birthday calls for a special birthday libation. Care to join me, Stanley? You only live once.

STANLEY. I don't drink, Maurice.

MAURICE. Well, sometimes people change.

STANLEY. I haven't changed yet.

MAURICE. Colleen?

COLLEEN. The baby's underage, Maurice, but thanks anyway.

HARRIET. I'll help you out, Maurice. I hate to see people drinkin' alone.

MAURICE. I appreciate that, Harriet. (*He pours HARRIET a glass and toasts.*) To a new age...a new era...a new epoch. And, to Colleen...for a happy and healthy future. May you find peace and contentment.

COLLEEN. That's very thoughtful, Maurice.

STANLEY. Maurice?

MAURICE. Yes, Stanley?

STANLEY. Age...era...and epoch are...ah...different terms.

MAURICE. But they all share the same backyard, don't they?

STANLEY. In a manner of speaking, they do.

COLLEEN. What are you taking notes for, Stanley?

STANLEY. I'm writing an article "A Look Back at Four Way." That's the title. We've got to know the past...so we'll know where to go in the future.

HARRIET (*swigging down the champagne*). It's all gonna change! After the stop sign there'll be a video store then a 7-Eleven or a 12 to 12. We'll have more conveniences than we'll know what to do with. But it still better be people. That's all there really is. Least should be, anyway. Colleen, you come back for a visit...you can stay with me and Victor. Thanks for the drink, Maurice. My granddaddy used to wear spats like that. (*HARRIET pauses and looks around.*) God! What a life. (*She exits. COLLEEN moves off to one side and looks at a spot on the horizon only she can see. We hear the honking of a car horn.*)

STANLEY. It's important. Someone has to keep records. Time makes us forget.

MAURICE. She knows, Stanley. Life looks confusing half way through it sometimes, that's all.

(*BOBBY JAMES DOBBINS enters. He is a little rough around the edges...moody...restless. He brings an air of considerable chaos with him. He is holding several dollars in his hand.)*

BOBBY JAMES *(talking rapidly).* You seen that? Pulled right in front of me. Where the hell do they come from? Old people really get me. Shouldn't be allowed to drive. Present company not included, Maurice.

MAURICE. That's charitable, Bobby James.

BOBBY JAMES. Hi, there, Colleen.

COLLEEN. Hello, Bobby James.

BOBBY JAMES. Where's Cheryl Mae? She been here? I forgot the damn laundry. She coulda brung it with her. Why do I have to do everything all the…*(Counting money.)* forty…sixty…eighty…damn, it's really building up. Another two hundred and sixty-five and I got me a real pickup. Damn Chevy's killing me. Shocks are gone. Gas is eatin' me alive. Hey, lemonade! Great idea. Gonna be a bitch today. Radio says it's gonna burn us up alive. What you all dressed up for, Maurice? Want some lemonade? *(Drinking.)* Not sweet enough. Damn. It's never sweet enough.

MAURICE. Got to watch your teeth, Bobby James.

BOBBY JAMES. Where they goin', man? They just sit in my face. *(Laughs.)* Then it's off to Oklahoma City. Or maybe Kansas City…get two jobs…work in both states…drive back 'n forth. *(Laughs.)* Got lots of jobs for mechanics. Got a trade…you always eat. That's what my Daddy said. Gonna open me a video store. Watch all the free movies I want. Or a baseball card store. Got Daddy's collection. Worth a fortune. Ain't gonna sell those. Ever! *(There is a lull in BOBBY JAMES's speechmaking while he drinks more lemonade. For a moment it is totally silent.)* Boy, sure is quiet all of a sudden. That's the way it is in a small town. Nothing happens. Well, off to the bank. Gotta put it right in… start building interest. Mom used to put five dollars a week into the bank…each week…for Cheryl Mae's and my education. Really built up, too. *(Beat.)* But we had to bury 'em, didn't we?

MAURICE. Yes.

BOBBY JAMES. Had to put 'em under right 'n' proper, didn't we, Maurice?

MAURICE. You did the right thing, Bobby James.

BOBBY JAMES. Cost a lot. 'Sides, I can't take any more school stuff. Talk, talk, talk! That's all they do. Day after day. Not me. No way. Well, I'm outta here! *(Seeing the lemonade sign.)* Boy, that sign's sure dumb! *(Exits.)*

MAURICE. Did you ever talk that fast, Stanley?

STANLEY. It wasn't my fault, Maurice. If I hadn't been going to my mother's for her birthday that night…I still dream about it. And the truck…all smashed up…his father's hands still holding onto the wheel.

MAURICE *(searching for change in his pocket)*. I'll just put down a nickel and a penny for three cups. That'll please Jackson. He'd he disappointed if no one got his joke.

STANLEY. Somebody had to tell the…children. Shouldn't have to hear it from the sheriff. When Bobby James opened the door and I told him…he just looked at me. Didn't say a thing. Just looked at me and closed the door. Parents were coming home from watching Cheryl Mae play…basketball…had a cold that night…folks wanted her to stay at home…but she said she wanted to play. Scored twenty-three points. Big picture of her on the front page of the *Times Record* the next morning.

COLLEEN. You did the right thing, Stanley.

STANLEY. And the two people in the other car…

COLLEEN. From Wisconsin.

MAURICE. Yes, from Wisconsin. Didn't stop at the crossroads. Went right on through.

STANLEY. What were they doing on the road to Four Way?

COLLEEN. Taking a short cut probably. On the way to someplace else. Who knows how they find us.

STANLEY. Bobby James will never...forgive me. Drank all that lemonade...and didn't even say hello to me.

(GEORGIA and HAROLD SWEENEY enter. HAROLD has good eyesight but has difficulty hearing. GEORGIA, on the other hand, has trouble with her vision but hears everything with great clarity. They are dressed casually, he in traditional "Retired Florida" and wide brimmed hat, and she in mid-calf pedal pushers and a floral print blouse. She carries a sun umbrella. He has two aluminum deck chairs and a Scrabble game under his arm.)

GEORGIA. Is that you, Stanley Frank? Thought I recognized your voice. Good morning.

STANLEY. Good morning, Mrs. Sweeney.

HAROLD. Morning, Stanley.

GEORGIA. It's Stanley Frank, Harold.

HAROLD. I know it's Stanley Frank, Georgia. I just said hello to him.

GEORGIA. You keepin' records today, Stanley? Taking notes?

STANLEY. Yes, ma'am. It's a big day for Four Way. It's our...birthday. *(STANLEY exits suddenly.)*

GEORGIA. Good for you, Stanley. I always enjoy your articles.

HAROLD. He's gone, Georgia.

GEORGIA *(to HAROLD)*. Stanley just seems to disappear at times. Ever notice that? Who's here this morning, Harold?

(HAROLD begins to arrange a wooden crate and the deck chairs and set up the Scrabble board. He and GEORGIA will play intermittently throughout the rest of the act.)

HAROLD. Colleen's here. Morning, Colleen.

COLLEEN. Morning, Harold.

GEORGIA. Colleen. All ready to go? Anything we can do?

COLLEEN. Just a few hours left. I'm ready. Thank you, Georgia.

GEORGIA. It's a big adventure, isn't it? You have great courage.

MAURICE. Morning, Georgia.

GEORGIA. Why, good morning, Maurice. Harold, you didn't tell me Maurice was here.

MAURICE. You're looking lovely today.

GEORGIA. Do you have your spats on, Maurice? All dressed up?

MAURICE. They're the talk of the town.

GEORGIA. You always look so dashing when you dress up. Doesn't he, Harold?

HAROLD *(ignoring MAURICE)*. There's some shade over here, Georgia. Radio said it was going to be 130 degrees today. World's going to burn up. And Four Way'll blow away like the wind.

GEORGIA. Harold's a little cranky this morning.

HAROLD. Walk...walk...walk! Same damn thing day in... day out. Park in front of B & W Feeds. Then down the south side of Main Street past Bonnie's Boutique. Have to look in and see what's new. Nothing new on that window dummy in ten years! Boutique, my foot. Used to just be called a dress shop when Luella Quincy owned it.

COLLEEN. Times change, Harold.

HAROLD. Then it's Wilson's hardware on the right. Old buzzard's got a sale on chain saws. Just what I need, a chainsaw. Cross the street, and you run smack into Federal Savings and Loan! Damn near got plowed under in the big scandal.

GEORGIA. Maurice has lived here for ages, Harold. He doesn't need the Cook's tour.

HAROLD. Neither do I. Not every day.

GEORGIA. Walking is good for the complexion.

MAURICE. You're living proof of that, Georgia.

HAROLD (to MAURICE). What do you mean by that remark?

GEORGIA. Oh, Harold, we're just flirting. You ought to try it sometime. Good for what ails you.

HAROLD. Yeah? What's that?

GEORGIA. Just about everything, sweetheart.

(BOBBY JAMES enters with CHERYL MAE.)

BOBBY JAMES. I don't have time to go back and get your dumb dress. Paulie and me are goin' out to the...

CHERYL MAE. Paulie and I...

BOBBY JAMES. Paulie and *me* are goin' out to the quarry to go swimmin' and then I gotta get back for the six o'clock shift! And stop tellin' me what I can do.

MAURICE. Another lemonade, Bobby James?

BOBBY JAMES. I ain't got time!

CHERYL MAE. Say "No, thank you." And don't say ain't.

BOBBY JAMES. Damn it to hell! You keep telling me how to talk and what to say and I swear I'm outta this stupid town just like that and you'll be talkin' to yourself at night 'stead of to Mom and Dad and there won't be no one there to hear ya cry, you hear me! (BOBBY JAMES exits in anger taking a swipe at the balloons and kicking at the car seat. A long pause.)

GEORGIA. It's heating up something awful. Colleen, sweetheart, could you get us a little lemonade? Maybe Cheryl Mae would like some cool...

HAROLD. What can you make with three "E's," a "T and a "Z"? Will you look at this!! This is my last game, Georgia. You hear me?

GEORGIA. Harold, be considerate here. Think of someone else for a change. (*COLLEEN has moved to the lemonade cooler and has poured some lemonade. She brings it to CHERYL MAE.*)

CHERYL MAE. He talked to Mr. Benson. He won't loan the money for the pick-up. Mom's old Chevy won't make it. Bobby James needs another $500.00 down and the plant might lay off his shift at the end of the week. They have a sign up in the lobby. And people aren't renewing their newspaper subscriptions. He doesn't put it on their porches. Just tosses it anywhere out the window. He drives so fast. (*Beat.*) He didn't mean to be rude. (*CHERYL MAE suddenly begins to cry. MAURICE takes her to his seat on the bench and sets her down on his handkerchief. COLLEEN sits next to CHERYL MAE.*)

COLLEEN. This heat does something terrible to a person.

GEORGIA. Boils up all the emotions inside.

MAURICE. And change. Change takes energy...generates heat...unsettles a lot of people.

GEORGIA. It's hard to be a young person these days, isn't it, Harold?

HAROLD. I have the "Z" and not a triple letter for miles.

CHERYL MAE. Thank you. I'm fine.

GEORGIA (*looking hard at the Scrabble board*). Z-E-E-T? Harold, there's no word called zeet.

HAROLD. You're looking at it upside down. Tease. It spells tease.

GEORGIA *(with disgust)*. Tease is spelled T-E-A-S-E.

HAROLD. Shoulda married a preacher's daughter instead of a school teacher. Preacher's daughter would just smile and look the other way.

(VICTOR enters with DARYL. He speaks with a sense of focus we haven't seen before. He has taken his medication.)

VICTOR *(to DARYL)*. Used to look out over the jungle and mow down all the trees. Had to clear a perimeter around the camp or they'd fall on ya from the branches at night like monkeys. Couldn't hear 'em 'til their blades tickled your tonsils. Then you didn't hear no more of nothin'.

DARYL. Lucky you survived.

VICTOR. Nobody survived, buddy. Nobody. *(To ALL.)* Everybody...I want you to meet Daryl Sweetwood. Daryl's my friend. He's from Harrison. He and his buddy are bringing old Four Way to the brink of the 20th Century. *(He notices CHERYL MAE has been crying and moves quickly to her.)* You all right Cheryl Mae? Did Babcock make a move on ya?

COLLEEN. She's fine, Victor. Just the heat.

CHERYL MAE *(to DARYL)*. Would you like a little lemonade? You must be thirsty.

DARYL. Thanks. I sure would. *(CHERYL MAE gets DARYL some lemonade.)*

GEORGIA *(to DARYL)*. Mrs. Elaine Burmester runs a lovely notions store in Harrison. Do you know her, Mr. Sweetwood?

DARYL. Yes, ma'am. She's my aunt. She's had that store near on thirty years.

GEORGIA. Isn't that something, Harold? It's still a small world. Let's take a drive over and say hello tomorrow.

HAROLD. You got enough notions, Georgia, and they're all strange. Don't need any more. *(CHERYL MAE brings the lemonade to DARYL and they move away from the others. MAURICE continues to sip his champagne. COLLEEN watches CHERYL MAE and DARYL for a moment, then quietly exits.)*

DARYL. Thanks. *(Drinks the lemonade.)*

CHERYL MAE. I didn't make it...I just...

DARYL. Well, tastes good anyway.

VICTOR *(looking at the Scrabble board).* Three "E's," a "T" and the "Z!" And not a triple letter for miles. You're in deep shit, Harold. Toss 'em back and draw again. I'm checkin' out. *(He sits on the ground and assumes the lotus position.)*

DARYL *(nodding to VICTOR).* Is he okay?

CHERYL MAE. He got hurt in the war. We all look out for him.

DARYL. You live nearby?

CHERYL MAE. Out east where the road hooks to the left. Mom and Dad died in a car accident last year. That's why you're puttin' in the sign.

DARYL. Oh.

CHERYL MAE. I live with my brother.

DARYL. My dad never came back from Nam. I help Mom out. Stay with her. She hasn't quite got on her feet.

CHERYL MAE. Church folks got together after the accident. Maurice...Mr. Darcy...helped us sell the farm land. We couldn't work it. Not many people are going into farming anymore. But the house is paid off anyway. We get the social security assistance. Basketball team bought me a used car to get around in.

DARYL. That was nice.

CHERYL MAE. Yeah.

DARYL. You graduate?

CHERYL MAE. This is my last year coming up.

DARYL. Gonna play ball?

CHERYL MAE. I'd like to. I had to sit out last year.

DARYL. I'm gonna go to the community college in West Bend. Have to help my mom a little, then I'm off. Education is important or you end up knowing the same stuff over and over every day.

CHERYL MAE. I want to do that, too. Learn about the world. Real soon. Got to help Bobby James first, though. He's not doing too well. Mrs. Sweeney got me a subscription to *National Geographic* for Christmas. I save every one of them.

DARYL *(beat)*. Well, thanks for the lemonade. Better be gettin' back...pull my weight. *(Begins to exit.)*

GEORGIA *(to DARYL)*. How long will it take you to put in the sign, Daryl?

DARYL. Dig the hole...pour the cement...couple, three more hours, ma'am. Not very long.

VICTOR. How 'bout the "time capsule?"

DARYL. Time capsule?

VICTOR. Yeah, can you believe that?

DARYL. What time capsule.

HAROLD. Is it time yet?

VICTOR. This whole day's about Jackson wanting to sink some damn box in the center of the earth for the rest of eternity.

GEORGIA. To commemorate our birthday.

MAURICE. Four Way was discovered 167 years ago today.

VICTOR *(gesturing to the balloons)*. That's what all these are here for. Aren't they "festive"?

DARYL. Nobody told me about a time capsule.

CHERYL MAE. We're supposed to put things in the box. When it's opened in another 100 years the town will have an identity.

GEORGIA. Something of ourselves to let the future know who lived here.

HAROLD. Just look in the county tax records. I'm in there big as life!

(AMY LYNN PURDY enters. She carries a large metal box, and a multiquart thermos with extra lemonade in it and a poster announcing the First Christian Church garage sale. Greetings are exchanged.)

AMY LYNN. My, oh, my, oh, dear! It's soooo hot! Victor, could you...oh, you're busy. Could someone...

DARYL. I'll help you, ma'am. *(Helps AMY LYNN with her items.)*

AMY LYNN. Ma'am? Oh, my. Thank you. Ma'am! What is your name? Such courtesy.

DARYL. Daryl Sweetwood, ma'am.

MAURICE. Daryl is putting up the stop sign, Amy Lynn.

AMY LYNN. That's wonderful, isn't it? Harold, how are you today?

HAROLD. Just drew a "J"...two "A's"...a..."U" and a..."K."

AMY LYNN. My, but that sounds...challenging.

MAURICE. Is this the box, Amy Lynn?

AMY LYNN. Yes, I hope it's not too large. It has to withstand the test of time, that's what Jackson says.

VICTOR. He's a quick man with a phrase, I'll give him that.

AMY LYNN *(suddenly defensive)*. It's not easy trying to generate a little enthusiasm in this town, let me tell you! And it's not what you do that's important, it's that you do something. Make an effort. Make things different. Try. Got to try. This is going to be a wonderful town. Jackson says the Holiday Inn was on the phone to him last week. They'll be out here next Thursday. I've got our guest room at home all fixed up for them and I'm going to fix a nice pot roast.

VICTOR *(beat)*. Sorry. It's the heat talkin'.

AMY LYNN. Me, too. I'm sorry I snapped at you but you can't let...things...hold you back.

MAURICE. You're doing what's right, Amy Lynn.

GEORGIA. The lemonade's very refreshing, Amy Lynn. We've been sipping it all morning.

AMY LYNN. Thank you. I brought some more. Look! Someone's put down a few cents. Jackson will be so proud. Well...there's a garage sale over at the First Christian Church set for tomorrow morning. You all know that? Have you seen the poster? *(Holds up poster.)* Doesn't that just leap out at you? So if you have anything you want to get rid of...

(JACKSON enters hurriedly.)

VICTOR. Ask and you shall receive.

AMY LYNN *(to JACKSON)*. Oh, sweetheart. I brought the time capsule and the extra lemonade.

JACKSON. Any more balloons? These are drooping a little bit.

VICTOR. It's a thousand degrees out here, Jackson, 'course they're droopin'.

AMY LYNN. I forgot the balloons! I'm sorry, I'll go back and...

JACKSON. You can get the balloons after lunch.

AMY LYNN *(making a note in a small notepad)*. Yes. I can do that. After lunch.

JACKSON (*to ALL*). The reporter from the *Times Record* said she'll be over later this afternoon. We'll have to hold off putting in the time capsule, but we'll still make it before nightfall...

AMY LYNN (*overlapping*). If I don't make a list then I...

JACKSON. Just got off the phone with her. She has to photo-graph a prize bull over in...

AMY LYNN. I tend to forget...

JACKSON. And Channel 7 from Hilltop Valley said they'd come if they could but...

AMY LYNN. There's so much to do.

JACKSON (*beat*). Amy Lynn. Please.

AMY LYNN. Sorry, dear. Go right ahead.

DARYL. Mr. Purdy? I'll have to call in and check out about the box.

JACKSON. Why? It's a small box. Shouldn't be any problem. Just put it under the sign and pour some concrete over it. Simple enough.

VICTOR. You didn't check on the time machine, Jackson? We're out here roastin' like peanuts and you didn't...

DARYL. Yes, sir, but I'll have to call in anyway. Our work order didn't say anything about a box.

JACKSON (*changing strategies*). You boys ready for lunch? Gettin' hungry?

DARYL. Well, sir...I think...

JACKSON. Amy Lynn fixes the best sandwiches in the whole...

AMY LYNN. Oh, Jackson...I don't think I have the time...

JACKSON. 'Course you do, Amy Lynn. Just slice up some of that ham you fixed...

GEORGIA. Cheryl Mae was planning to take Daryl to the Oasis, weren't you, Cheryl Mae?

CHERYL MAE. Ah...

JACKSON *(reaching into his wallet)*. Is that right? Well, that's a good idea. Here, let me pick up the tab.

GEORGIA. It's our treat, Jackson. Isn't that right, Harold?

HAROLD. Who's a treat?

GEORGIA *(reaching into her purse)*. You are, darling. Now, when it's time, Cheryl Mae, you and Daryl...oh, what about your helper?

DARYL. Ah...he always brings his lunch. *(DARYL moves to the telephone on the tree.)* Let me just make that call.

GEORGIA. That doesn't work, I'm afraid.

JACKSON *(scornfully)*. 'Cept when God calls.

VICTOR. Take that tone outta your voice, Jackson.

MAURICE. You'll find one at the Oasis, Daryl.

DARYL. Thanks. Well, I'll be back in a bit, Cheryl Mae. *(To AMY LYNN.)* The lemonade's real fine, ma'am. *(DARYL exits.)*

AMY LYNN. So polite. Isn't he polite?

JACKSON. I had the money right here. It was no problem. Why doesn't anyone let me do something?

VICTOR. That's not how it's done, Jackson. You can't bribe people.

(HARRIET enters carrying a fan and a couple of crushed doll boxes.)

HARRIET. Who's going over to the church? I got this fan here for the garage sale...blade's bent. And these Ken and Barbie dolls. Mrs. Randall sat on them by mistake when Victor was puttin' the barbecue together.

JACKSON. Victor can straighten the fan out. Bang his head against it.

VICTOR. That's it! No more. *(Squaring off for a fight.)* Right here, Jackson.

JACKSON. You've been chewin' on my ass all morning and I've about had it!

VICTOR. I'll put parts of you in that stupid ass time capsule of yours. They can assemble you like an erector set and get an idea what a town jerk looked like in the old days!

AMY LYNN. Sweetheart, let's go home and...

VICTOR. You come in here thinkin' we're all dead. Well, we ain't dead. Sweat in my eyes...drops so big you could suck on 'em like sour balls...and Sally Louise and me and Ray Bob Jordan moving forward. Then the crickets stopped all at the same time. I had to take a crap so bad my hole was up around my neck. You've had that feeling a lot, I bet, haven't ya, Jackson? And then he stepped on it. And the top half of him went this way...and the bottom half just kinda...fell over. Plop. That's dead, Jackson. You wanna bring someone back from the dead...you bring back Jimmy Loon. And then the crickets started up again. They were all out of tune. Ever tell you about the crickets, Maurice?

MAURICE. Don't think you ever did, Victor.

VICTOR. Well sometime when we ain't got such a big day to deal with I'll tell you all about it. (*Exits.*)

MAURICE. I'll look forward to it.

GEORGIA. Victor never told that story before.

HAROLD. I typed up lists. The captain gave me lists of things and I typed them up. Spent four years in North Carolina. That's all I did in WWII. No crickets 'cept at night when I had guard duty. Nothing to guard 'cept a warehouse full of typewriters. Doesn't seem fair.

JACKSON. The balloons and the lemonade...they're symbols...a new time in our lives. What's wrong with that? We've got to make something grow here!

HARRIET. You're movin' too fast. Have some lemonade. I hear it's good.

JACKSON. Can't just live each day and then die when it's over?

MAURICE. Been doing it for centuries.

JACKSON. Have to leave something behind.

(COLLEEN enters carrying several dresses, an evening cape, and some shoes.)

COLLEEN. Went back to the house. Forgot the upstairs closet. Guess you just put things outta your mind. Found a few things you might like, Cheryl Mae.

CHERYL MAE. Oh, I couldn't wear those, Colleen. They're too pretty.

COLLEEN. Dress pretty…you'll think pretty. My mother told me that and she was the prettiest woman I've ever seen. Here, try these shoes on. You can wear this cape on Halloween. *(CHERYL MAE begins trying on a pair of shoes.)*

HARRIET. That's nice of you, Colleen.

COLLEEN. I've had it with party dresses and good times, Harriet. I've had it with followin' men around…waitin' to be told.

AMY LYNN. Gonna marry again?

COLLEEN. Maybe. Maybe not. It's not the answer to everything, I'll tell you that.

AMY LYNN. Where are you going?

COLLEEN. I've got friends in South Carolina. I'll go there for a while. Or maybe out west. I don't really know.

HAROLD. Go west young man! What a crock! Nothing but freeways and earthquakes.

GEORGIA. Harold, be polite.

AMY LYNN. How about the baby?

COLLEEN. I'll have it at my folks' place. *(Beat.)* I'm scared.

HARRIET. You'll do fine. Don't cave in now.

COLLEEN. I don't know if I'm doin' the right thing.

HARRIET. Nobody does. It's all a big guess.

JACKSON. Hey, now. Everybody. Cheer up! What are you going to put in the time capsule? I've got a list of the names of all the town officials and a list of our churches.

AMY LYNN. The First Christian and the Free Will Baptist.

HARRIET. Variety is the spice of life, I'll give ya that.

HAROLD. I'll put this damn Scrabble board in that time capsule, that's what I'll do.

GEORGIA. Now, Harold…

HAROLD. Three "O's"! And a "Q"…and a "J"! J-O-O-O-Q. Joke!

GEORGIA. What are you leaving for posterity, Cheryl Mae?

CHERYL MAE. I'm not for sure but I think maybe a picture of Mom and Dad and where they worked. And were born.

GEORGIA. Maurice?

MAURICE. My wedding picture. And a copy of the poem I put next to Margaret before they buried her.

GEORGIA. I brought a letter my father wrote me from Korea three days before he died.

COLLEEN. I think I'll put in a copy of my divorce papers.

HAROLD. Give me another hour and I'll put mine in there, too.

GEORGIA. Amy Lynn?

AMY LYNN. Oh, I wouldn't know. Jackson hasn't decided yet.

JACKSON. When the reporter from the *Times Record* shows up we'll all line up for a group shot so we can make the front page. Maybe they'll pick it up on the wire service and put it on *Time* magazine!

HARRIET. Hell of an idea, Jackson. You'll be mayor before the sun sets. Bring those dresses over to the store, Cheryl Mae, and you can try them on for size. I'll leave Ken and

Barbie here with the rest of you beautiful people. Save me a seat. I don't want to miss the 21st Century. *(Exits.)*

JACKSON. So much to do and nothing's turning out right.

AMY LYNN. I'll get more balloons, sweetheart.

JACKSON *(beginning to exit. Carrying the "time capsule").* Good, more balloons…and then we'll put…everything…in the time capsule. This is great fun, isn't it? You look a lot like my grandfather, Maurice, dressed up like that. *(Exits.)*

MAURICE *(beat).* Care to join me for lunch, Harold? Georgia? It's too hot to stay out here much longer. Then maybe a little poker later this afternoon. You up for a little poker, Harold?

HAROLD. I knew it! I knew you couldn't go the whole day without mentioning that card game.

MAURICE. Georgia, did I mention any specific card game?

GEORGIA *(gathering up her items).* He's very sensitive on that issue, Maurice.

HAROLD. I kept four cards.

GEORGIA. The Ace…King…Queen…and Jack of Spades. Yes, we know, Harold.

HAROLD. A Royal flush! In one more card. A Royal flush! I've never had a Royal flush.

GEORGIA. And Maurice kept a pair of sevens, didn't you, Maurice?

HAROLD. I was there, Georgia! I don't need a history lesson.

MAURICE *(assisting GEORGIA by taking her arm).* That's right Georgia. I kept a pair of sevens and drew three more cards. And Harold drew his fifth card.

GEORGIA. You bet the farm, didn't you, Harold? On the three of diamonds.

MAURICE. Tried to bluff me out. Almost folded my sevens, as I recall. Glad I didn't.

HAROLD. Sixty bucks! You cost me sixty bucks! A pair of sevens!

GEORGIA. Maybe another day for lunch, Maurice.

HAROLD. Stay away from my wife, you card shark!

GEORGIA. See you after lunch, Colleen?

COLLEEN. I'll be here. *(GEORGIA and HAROLD exit.)*

(STANLEY enters carrying two large building stones.)

STANLEY. Where is...everybody? Look...see...right here.

CHERYL MAE. What are they, Stanley?

STANLEY. Building stones, I think.

MAURICE. They look rounded. Both the same size.

STANLEY. This is amazing! Where do I put these? We shouldn't dig anymore. I can't put them down.

MAURICE. Of course, you can, Stanley. They won't go any-where.

STANLEY. No, I have to feel the history. Touch them. Go ahead. They're very special. See? *(COLLEEN, CHERYL MAE and MAURICE dutifully touch the stones. AMY LYNN hesitates and then touches them.)*

MAURICE. Feels like history to me. What do you think, Amy Lynn?

AMY LYNN. What are we supposed to do now!?

STANLEY *(as if seeing a vision)*. See them? All sitting around the family table. At sunset time. The fields all quiet and waiting for the rain.

AMY LYNN. I don't see anything.

COLLEEN. Stanley, how about some lunch?

STANLEY. No time for lunch. I looked down into the hole and...Maurice, there's a whole row of them. Have to get back. *(STANLEY exits with the stones still in his hands.)*

(BOBBY JAMES enters in a high state of anxiety.)

BOBBY JAMES. Damn car! Been walking for the last half hour. Nothin' works anymore! Take me to the quarry, Cheryl Mae. Gotta get a…thing…for the engine. And I gotta get out to the quarry. How am I gonna get to work?

CHERYL MAE. The quarry's not safe. Mom told you never to go to the…

BOBBY JAMES. I can do what I want. Mom's not here anymore! Gimme your keys.

CHERYL MAE. I'll take you to work. But I won't take you to the quarry.

BOBBY JAMES. What about lunch?

CHERYL MAE. I'm having lunch with Daryl.

BOBBY JAMES. You gonna go out with him tonight?

CHERYL MAE. Maybe.

BOBBY JAMES. You gonna do things?

COLLEEN. That's not attractive talk, Bobby James. Might as well learn that now. Some women are attracted to it. Basic types are what I call 'em. Your mom and dad brought you up better. Be nice to your sister. She's all you've got now. You meet in the middle here and work things out.

BOBBY JAMES. Everybody tells me what to do! I got to get out of here! *(Exits quickly.)*

COLLEEN. Cheryl Mae, you take that young man to lunch now and take these dresses with you. Stop by Harriet's like she said and try them on after lunch.

CHERYL MAE. Thank you, Colleen. They're lovely. They really are…*(CHERYL MAE exits quickly carrying the dresses with her.)*

MAURICE. Would you ever want to be his age again, Colleen?

COLLEEN. You mean with all that energy and vitality and spirit and power? You bet I would.

MAURICE. I was referring to his state of anxiety.

AMY LYNN. I wish I could help him. He seems so…frightened.

COLLEEN. Come on, Maurice. My treat today. The Oasis Blue Plate special. I'll serve ya myself.

MAURICE. I'd like that, Colleen. Thank you. Must be the spats.

COLLEEN. You're welcome, too, Amy Lynn. It's too hot for humans out here.

AMY LYNN. It's quiet now. I like to gather my thoughts. It's not that hot, really. I don't mind the heat. I've got the balloons to get up and I have to take the fan and Ken and Barbie over to…

MAURICE. I'll take everything over after lunch. You rest now.

AMY LYNN. Thank you just the same. I don't mind.

COLLEEN. Suit yourself.

MAURICE. I don't know what this time capsule is going to tell the future about Four Way. We all seem a little out of focus if you ask me. *(COLLEEN and MAURICE exit. AMY LYNN sits under the tree. She is exhausted. She straightens up the lemonade stand, picks up a gum wrapper or two.)*

(After a few moments, JACKSON enters. He is carrying a chain saw.)

JACKSON. You go on and get the balloons now, Amy Lynn.

AMY LYNN. Do you know how to use that, Jackson?

JACKSON. Just pull this thing here. Hurry along now.

AMY LYNN. No.

JACKSON. Have to do it, Amy Lynn. Nothin's workin' out like it should. You want something done right, you have to do it yourself. Should have known that all along.

AMY LYNN. No.

JACKSON. You go on now.

AMY LYNN. Don't do this, sweetheart. Please.

JACKSON. I'll be home in a minute. Make me one of your famous sandwiches.

AMY LYNN. They won't be famous anymore if you cut down this tree, Jackson. We'll have to leave. I don't want to leave.

JACKSON. I'll be right along. *(AMY LYNN exits. He tries to start the chain saw but it won't work.)* Damn! Nothin' works in this town. *(In frustration he raises the chain saw as if to hack at the tree when the telephone on the tree begins to ring. He freezes.)*

END ACT ONE

ACT TWO

AT RISE: *The time is early evening around 7:30. HAROLD and VICTOR are engaged in a poker game. CHERYL MAE is pacing. GEORGIA is sifting through a variety of white goods she is donating to the church garage sale. HARRIET is fanning herself with a large wicker fan and drinking a beer from the six-pack that sits next to her on the ground. Several of the rounded stones STANLEY found earlier are visible. Pre-sunset colors define the rather tranquil tableau.*

VICTOR (*shuffling and dealing the cards*). Okay! Here we go! Gotta get you retooled for the rematch. Seven card stud. Two down…four up…and the last one down.

HAROLD. Young man, I was playing poker before you could find your pecker!

GEORGIA. Don't be vulgar, Harold.

VICTOR. Yeah, Harold. That's my job.

HAROLD. You have all the fun.

GEORGIA. Harold insisted on a drink after our nap.

HAROLD. Have to get through the day, don't I?

GEORGIA. You know better.

HAROLD. I know how to get through the day!

GEORGIA. "It's too hot to drink, alcohol, Harold," I said.

HAROLD. That's what she said. What a memory. Says it every day.

GEORGIA. Went home for lunch. Harold didn't want to eat with Maurice.

HAROLD. Maurice is a cheater. Won't eat with cheaters.

GEORGIA. So I fixed a delightful lettuce and tomato sandwich, didn't I, Harold?

HAROLD. I'm not a rabbit, Georgia.

VICTOR. I had a bag of Doritos. Washed 'em down with three cans of Mountain Dew.

HARRIET. They don't call you Mister Nutrition for nothing, that's for sure.

CHERYL MAE. I told Bobby James not to go. Why did he have to jump into the water?

VICTOR. All the guys were standin' around watchin'. A dare's a dare. He had to do it.

HAROLD. Can't lose face.

VICTOR. Those are the rules.

HARRIET *(to VICTOR)*. That's a hell of a philosophy. You'd lay down in front of stampedin' buffalo if someone paid you, wouldn't you?

VICTOR. How much ya got on ya?

CHERYL MAE. He doesn't take care of himself.

GEORGIA. He's got you for now, Cheryl Mae. You do a wonderful job. Come over here and help me fold these, will you, dear?

CHERYL MAE. What's he goin' to do when he goes to college?

VICTOR. There's lots of Doritos in the world.

GEORGIA. He'll look up one day and see the way. Don't you worry.

HAROLD. I hear that crap everyday. Can you imagine that! "Harold, you'll look up one day and see the way"!

GEORGIA. Harold, be civil.

HAROLD (*to VICTOR*). You going to bet? You're high. Ten of hearts. It's your bet.

VICTOR. You're trackin' just fine, Harold, old boy. Ten cents.

HAROLD. Ten cents!

VICTOR. Ten cents on the ten of hearts. Ain't she sweet?

HAROLD (*putting his bet on the table*). Shut up and deal. I ain't gonna live forever!

VICTOR (*dealing another round*). Oh, lookee here! Pair of tens! A quarter, Harold.

HAROLD. A quarter! I'll have to take out a loan.

GEORGIA. Then Harold wanted to stop in at the Oasis, didn't you, sweetheart?

HAROLD. I was thirsty! Wanted to play some pool.

VICTOR. How'd ya do?

HAROLD. Lost.

VICTOR. Who'd ya play?

HAROLD. Myself.

GEORGIA. I wrote three letters and did a crossword puzzle.

HAROLD. Doesn't that sound like a fascinating afternoon?

GEORGIA. I had to keep an eye on you.

VICTOR. Can't let the good ones get away, right, Georgia?

HARRIET. My, oh my, Georgia, what we do for love.

(*MAURICE enters.*)

MAURCIE. He'll be fine, Cheryl Mae. After he got fixed up he just tore out of the driveway. Thought I should follow him. He didn't get very far. Can't get around much with his engine conking out like that.

CHERYL MAE. Where was he?

MAURICE. Out by the cemetery. He was crying.

CHERYL MAE. He was talking to Mom and Dad.

MAURICE. But he's all better now. I'll tow it back in tomorrow. Shouldn't be much to get it fixed. He's not in a very good frame of mind, though.

BOBBY JAMES (*off*). Ow. Damn!

CHERYL MAE (*calling off*). Bobby James?

BOBBY JAMES (*off*). I'm coming…I'm coming.

(BOBBY JAMES enters. His arm is in a sling and he walks with a limp.)

GEORGIA. Sit down, Bobby James. Right over here by me.

BOBBY JAMES. I'm okay. No big deal. I'm fine. (*CHERYL MAE helps BOBBY JAMES to the bench.*) I can do it. It's just my ankle. Let me do it.

HARRIET. What did Doc Williams give you?

BOBBY JAMES. Some stuff.

HARRIET. Let me see. (*BOBBY JAMES hands two pill bottles to HARRIET who gives her approval and hands them to CHERYL MAE.*) Be sure he takes these just like they say. One's gonna make him sleepy…the other's for…

BOBBY JAMES. I can't sleep! Lost my damn job. Shoulda given me your car! I gotta get some work. I gotta get outta here!

CHERYL MAE. If you hadn't jumped off the bluffs you'd been to work on time and you'd have your silly job back! I get so mad at you sometimes. Everybody's helpin' us out and you just…

BOBBY JAMES. Quit raggin' on me, Cheryl Mae!

VICTOR. Shit happens.

BOBBY JAMES. Yeah!

VICTOR. Us guys know how it is, don't we, Tiger?

BOBBY JAMES. Guess so, yeah.

VICTOR. Gotta stick together.

HARRIET. Shut up and deal, Victor.

HAROLD. When we were kids we used to jump off movin' trains. Pick 'em up leaving the stockyards then jump off just after they turned the bend heading north outta town. Now that was exciting. Got chicken once...hung on for forty miles. Just couldn't let go. Wet my pants. Got off at the next stop and hid behind the luggage wagon until I could pick one up comin' back home. Got in at 1:30 in the morning. My mother wasn't too happy about that.

HARRIET. You were a real Tarzan, weren't you, Harold?

HAROLD. Told my friends I'd spent the day in jail with a man who murdered his whole family, chopped 'em into little pieces and ate 'em with ketchup.

VICTOR. Way to go, Harold.

GEORGIA *(to HAROLD)*. You're an awful man!

HAROLD. Word got around school pretty fast. Boys each paid a penny to hear me tell the story. I'd tell a few of 'em at lunch time...and a few of 'em after school.

GEORGIA. Never the same story.

HAROLD. Had to keep up their interest.

GEORGIA. By the end of the week it was Harold who had killed the man in jail, poured ketchup all over his body and served him up in tiny pieces to Harold's parents for Sunday supper. The story stopped after the principal called his mother.

HAROLD. But by the time the week was over I'd made enough money to buy me a muffler and some mittens. Best job I ever had.

GEORGIA. Is there a moral to this story, Harold?

HAROLD. Hell, yes!

GEORGIA. What is it?

HAROLD. I'm workin' on it! It's coming to me!

MAURICE *(to BOBBY JAMES).* I called the plant. Told them you injured yourself trying to save another boy from drowning. They said to come in tomorrow if you're up to it. *(Beat.)* And they said they were proud of you.

GEORGIA. Maurice, you didn't.

MAURICE. No real harm done, Georgia. Just a little white lie.

HAROLD. You can make some big money with that story, Bobby James. 'Course you'll have to split it 60-40 with your drowned friend. *(To VICTOR.)* Up a quarter. I feel like a winner! Deal, dammit. I'm working on a Chinese straight.

VICTOR *(dealing).* Three tens. A full house arisin'. Fifty cents, Harold, or I take your wife as collateral.

HAROLD. I'm flat broke. She's yours.

CHERYL MAE. Thank you, Mr. Darcy. Bobby James?

BOBBY JAMES. Yeah, thanks, Maurice.

HARRIET. Well, that's over and behind us. What's next on the dance card, I wonder?

(STANLEY enters carrying a copy of the Times Record.*)*

HARRIET. Hello, Stanley. Wanna dance? Guess not.

STANLEY. Is everybody here?

VICTOR. Who's here is here, Stanley.

STANLEY. Jackson says…oh, this is wrong. We have to get everything straightened out. It's the tree…

VICTOR. Calm down, Stanley and finish a sentence, for God's sake. Just one sentence, okay? *(STANLEY begins to hyperventilate.)*

HARRIET. Stanley, you're gonna float right up off the ground if you keep doin' that.

GEORGIA. What's the matter, Stanley?

HAROLD. Probably saw my hand.

STANLEY. The hole in the ground.

GEORGIA. What hole?

HAROLD. The stop sign, Georgia! Stay awake.

HARRIET. Stanley, you've been working too hard. Calm down now. It's been a long, hot day.

STANLEY. That young man called his boss about the time capsule…to make it wider…for the box. And now the tree. They held a meeting.

GEORGIA. What meeting, Stanley? It's hard to follow you.

STANLEY. Jackson and the others. They had a meeting. But I had to fix lunch for Mother. I should have been at the meeting. *(Reading from the paper.)* Here see? It's in the business section. "Friday, August 13, 1993. National Bank Board Room. 2:30 P.M." Mother called and said she didn't feel up to…

VICTOR. Keep reading, Stanley.

STANLEY. "In attendance: Jackson Purdy, Winston Radford…"

HARRIET. Winston Radford?

MAURICE. Real estate developer from…

HARRIET. I know everybody in this town, Maurice! I've never heard of any Winston Radford.

STANLEY. "…Elizabeth Hammond…"

HARRIET. Who the hell is Elizabeth Hammond?

MAURICE. She's Winston Radford's associate.

HARRIET. I don't like so many people comin' into our town. It's not their town. It's ours!

MAURICE. It's progress, Harriet.

STANLEY *(with more focus and strength than we've seen so far).* I want to finish! Let me finish! You ask me questions and then…you…don't listen to my answers!

GEORGIA. We're very sorry, Stanley. It's rude of us. Harold, be attentive.

BOBBY JAMES. Who cares about some old meeting?

CHERYL MAE. This is no time to talk, Bobby James. This is important.

HAROLD. Get on with it, Stanley. I got him on the ropes here.

STANLEY *(referring to the newspaper)*. Wally Steers was there, too.

HARRIET. B and B Feed Store. His prices are a little steep for my blood. *(Beat.)* Sorry. Go ahead, Stanley.

STANLEY. Jack Billingsly, Bubba Morrison and Roger Gossett.

HARRIET. Who are these people? They never shop in my store. This is gettin' outta hand.

STANLEY. They're shareholders in the Skyways Natural Gas Company. I go to the meetings when I can. They usually just have lunch, talk about drilling wells, buying up land. But nothing really happens. Just a lot of talk. But I had to fix Mother's lunch.

GEORGIA. You do a wonderful job, Stanley.

VICTOR. Get on with it, Stanley, or we'll be here 'til hell freezes over!

STANLEY. Don't you talk down to me! Just because you went to war and I couldn't go...don't you talk down to me! I deal with important things, too. What if I didn't keep up with history?

HARRIET. How 'bout a cold beer, Stanley?

MAURICE. Maybe some lemonade, Harriet.

HARRIET *(moving toward the lemonade)*. Lemonade. Good idea, Maurice.

STANLEY *(blurting out the news)*. They're going to cut down the tree. Then there'll be nothing left.

HAROLD *(beat).* Tree?

GEORGIA. They wouldn't.

HAROLD. What tree?

MAURICE. This tree, I think, Harold. Am I correct, Stanley? *(STANLEY nods.)*

BOBBY JAMES. They can cut the whole place down, as far as I'm concerned.

CHERYL MAE. Shush up!

STANLEY. Make the street wider for the customers of the future. More people coming. More things to do. *(Pointing.)* A right turn lane over there. *(Looking at the newspaper again.)* "To bring the 21st Century to our doorstep."

GEORGIA. Cut down the tree?

STANLEY. All those sleeping people at the Ramada Inn. That's what Jackson says.

VICTOR. There ain't no Ramada Inn! Just that silly ass Night Night Motel out on the highway.

HARRIET. Do we have capital punishment in this state?

(JACKSON enters quietly with AMY LYNN a few steps behind. There is a considerable silence. AMY LYNN is carrying a bag of fireworks and chicken wrapped in aluminum foil.)

AMY LYNN. I brought some fried chicken in case anyone is hungry. The reporter from the *Times Record* called. Running late. Will be here for the fireworks, though. See? We brought some fireworks for later.

VICTOR. There's gonna be some fireworks...you're right there, lady.

HARRIET. Think we lost our appetite, Amy Lynn.

STANLEY. I told 'em about the tree, Jackson.

AMY LYNN. Maybe later then.

GEORGIA. That's a good idea *(AMY LYNN puts the fire-works and the chicken near the tree.)*

JACKSON. I'm glad it's out in the open. Good.

VICTOR. You don't quite get the picture, do you, city boy?

MAURICE. It's not a popular decision, Jackson.

GEORGIA. This tree's been here before the Wright brothers flew up into the clouds.

HAROLD. So have you, Georgia.

GEORGIA. Now now, Harold!

HARRIET. I don't think we can let you do this, Jackson.

JACKSON. Those meetings are open to everyone. You all have an opportunity to voice your opinion. We put up announcements in the bank.

HAROLD. Who can afford to go to the bank these days!

JACKSON. And in the newspaper.

VICTOR. Newspaper? Hell, ain't nothin' around here worth readin' about.

HARRIET. No one's showed up to any meetings in twenty years.

JACKSON. All that's changing, Harriet. It's all legal. We met. We voted. We agreed.

GEORGIA. Voted? Who voted?

HARRIET. Agreed? Who agreed? Who gave you the authority to call a meeting anyway?

JACKSON. We're looking down the road, Harriet. We're shaping destiny.

VICTOR. Did you ask the tree, Jackson? Ever ask the tree if it wanted to end up as firewood?

JACKSON. Look at it. The limbs are dead...the leaves are dying...like this town.

GEORGIA. Needs a little rain is all. That's what we all need, I think.

HAROLD. The Indians used to camp here after they hunted the buffalo. I read that in one of Stanley's articles.

MAURICE. This is where Margaret and I came to watch the sunset, Jackson. For years and years.

HAROLD. Where would we play Scrabble?

AMY LYNN. We're planning a Senior Center activity schedule with trips to the Harrison mall and...

VICTOR. Lucky you, Harold. I can't wait to get old around here! Yessiree!

BOBBY JAMES. Cut it down! The buffalo are gone. The whole place is dead. Who gives a crap?

GEORGIA (*forcefully*). I do, young man. I give a big crap!

HAROLD. Believe her, boy. She gives a big crap.

JACKSON. You all make me sick.

AMY LYNN. Sweetheart, I don't think...

VICTOR (*moving toward JACKSON*). Those may have been your last words, Jackson. Write those down, Stanley. A day in history.

JACKSON. It's a lousy tree! And a lousy hole in the ground.

STANLEY. See those rocks? They fit. They fit together. It's not just a lousy hole in the...(*Placing the rocks next to each other.*) See? People lived here.

GEORGIA. What are you saying, Stanley?

STANLEY. Samuel Kingsley Wilson!

VICTOR. Who the hell is Samuel Kingsley Wilson?

HARRIET. He doesn't shop in my store either.

MAURICE. He's why we're here, Harriet.

STANLEY (*pulling out several pages of his drafted article on the history of Four Way*). It's all part of my article. "Born in 1803...in Lords Town, Scotland, Samuel Kingsley Wilson and his wife, Louise, and their three sons, Aaron, Caleb and Mitchell..."

VICTOR. Beers, anyone? This could take a while. (*VICTOR pulls a beer out of HARRIET's six pack.*)

STANLEY. "...and their daughter Clarissa, arrived in America in 1847."

JACKSON. It's over, Stanley. That's all in the past. We're here now!!

HARRIET. Let him be, Jackson.

STANLEY. "After several months Samuel and his family settled outside Twin Forks, Ohio on the Ohio river."

JACKSON. We met. We agreed.

STANLEY. "He was a boat maker and also made leather coats for trappers and frontiersmen."

JACKSON. The street needs to be wider!

STANLEY. No! You can't. Letters say his house was built of stone near the path where two trees met above the trail... like a roof! I have gone through all the records in the library. And I'm right.

JACKSON (*moving around the setting*). I don't see another tree, do you? Does anyone? Not another tree for miles. Go ahead. Point to a tree. I don't even see a tree stump!

BOBBY JAMES. I'm with Jackson! Who cares about dead people anyway? They ain't ever comin' back.

CHERYL MAE. You close your mouth tight! You hear me? I am so tired of picking up after you. Fixing you this and fixing you that...waiting for you to grow up! How dare you talk about Mommy and Daddy that way!

BOBBY JAMES. I can say what I want. Did you hear that!! I can't wait to get out of here. (*He sits on the ground behind the tree trunk.*)

STANLEY (*yelling*). We can't let it all fall away! Can't let concrete cover up our lives! Doesn't anybody care? Nobody listens to me.

MAURICE (*overlapping*). We appreciate all you...

STANLEY. We're the last moment on earth.

VICTOR. Amen!

STANLEY. Evolution standing at the edge of time itself!

HARRIET. That's a little scary.

HAROLD. He's gonna blow a gasket!

STANLEY. Years upon years of travail and sorrow...

MAURICE. Stanley, don't get so excited.

BOBBY JAMES. Let's have a party! Time to celebrate! Happy. Birthday!!! *(BOBBY JAMES has found the fire-crackers and lights them. When STANLEY hears the explosions he slumps to the ground.)*

CHERYL MAE. Bobby James!

HARRIET *(moving quickly to STANLEY's side)*. Stanley? Someone, get some lemonade. Quick. *(CHERYL MAE moves to the lemonade stand.)* Dammit, Bobby James. I ought to put you over my knee and...

(LUCINDA HARRIS enters. She wears a backpack and stands on the fringe of the action and watches.)

VICTOR *(reacting to the loud sounds)*. Incoming...incoming! Medic! Medic! *(VICTOR takes cover. He is professional, very quick, and very serious. He moves to BOBBY JAMES and forces him to the ground. The dialogue is frantic and overlapping.)*

BOBBY JAMES. Hey, leave me alone. What the hell are you...hey...stop this!

VICTOR. Stay low, boy.

MAURICE. Victor, there's no need to...

VICTOR. Head down, kid. Over this way. *(BOBBY JAMES escapes VICTOR's grasp. VICTOR does a "low crawl" and ducks behind the sofa.)*

HARRIET. Heartbeat's strong! Get his feet up. Amy Lynn! *(MAURICE helps HARRIET with STANLEY. AMY LYNN gets a picnic blanket and puts it under STANLEY's head.)* His feet are at the other end, Amy Lynn.

AMY LYNN *(referring to VICTOR)*. He scares me!

VICTOR *(to AMY LYNN)*. Get down, woman. You wanna die?

GEORGIA. Victor, we're not in danger! This is Four Way!

BOBBY JAMES. This is great. What a zoo!

VICTOR *(moving to STANLEY who has begun to come around)*. You stay down low, buddy. We'll get you out of here. This ain't friendly fire. Everybody spread out. Stay down.

STANLEY. Can't let them...cut down the tree.

VICTOR *(to HAROLD)*. Cover the left flank, soldier.

HAROLD *(to JACKSON)*. See what you've down? We were fine until you drove up in your foreign car. If you'd bought American everything woulda been fine. We ought to string you up by your thumbs like they used to in the old West!

JACKSON. It's just a stop sign.

AMY LYNN. We never fit in. No matter where we are. Things just don't work out.

JACKSON. It's just a tree! I'll plant fifty more trees anywhere you want.

HARRIET. Water! A towel. A shirt. Something! Let's move it, troops. *(CHERYL MAE and GEORGIA go to the folded clothes and select an old towel and a shirt and bring them to HARRIET who dries STANLEY's forehead.)*

MAURICE. Stay calm, Stanley. Everything is fine. I think everyone's safe now.

AMY LYNN. Jackson, don't just stand there! Help us.

BOBBY JAMES. Should I take a picture of this for the time capsule? *(He gets STANLEY's Polaroid and takes several pictures. LUCINDA continues to watch the activity.)*

AMY LYNN. Jackson! If you don't help us, I'll leave you. Do you hear me! *(JACKSON doesn't move for a moment then goes to the lemonade stand and fetches some lemonade and gives it to AMY LYNN who gives it to STANLEY who takes a sip.)*

(COLLEEN enters carrying two hat boxes for the garage sale.)

COLLEEN. I heard gun shots.

BOBBY JAMES. Gun shots! That's great!

MAURICE. They were firecrackers. We were celebrating. Stanley brought history to Four Way.

COLLEEN. Must have been some effort.

STANLEY *(more clearly now)*. He built a reputation as a...he came to Four Way in 1873...1832...it's all gone! I can't remember.

MAURICE. It'll come back to you, Stanley.

STANLEY. I've forgotten our history.

GEORGIA. You fainted, that's all. You'll be fine. *(The tempo settles down a bit. COLLEEN puts down her garage sale items.)*

STANLEY. His daughter married...a man from...*(STANLEY begins to search for his papers which have been strewn over the area. LUCINDA steps in and picks up several sheets.)*

AMY LYNN *(to JACKSON)*. Nobody likes us here, Jackson.

JACKSON. People like us fine, Amy Lynn, and that's the end of it!

AMY LYNN. I try so hard but nobody likes us. I even buy things through the catalogues just so I'll have something to give away at garage sales. We'll end up giving everything away and they still won't like us.

MAURICE *(seeing LUCINDA for the first time)*. Hello.

LUCINDA. Hi.

STANLEY *(trying to rise to his feet)*. Have to get back to the…

HARRIET. Not quite yet, Stanley. Did you eat today?

VICTOR. You got to eat, Stanley. Learned that this morning. I got some Doritos over here somewhere.

AMY LYNN *(giving STANLEY a piece of chicken)*. I have some chicken.

LUCINDA *(taking off her backpack)*. I've got some crackers in here. And a couple of cans of fruit cocktail.

STANLEY. I think I'm better now.

CHERYL MAE *(to LUCINDA)*. Hi.

LUCINDA. Hi. What happened?

GEORGIA. The heat in this world is something fierce. That's what happened. Just takes a body's brain away.

VICTOR. I got to check back into the V.A., Harriet. Can't keep doin' this. It's anti-social. *(Sees LUCINDA.)* Hello, hello, hello! My heart, my heart!

LUCINDA. Hi.

JACKSON *(checking to see if he is presentable)*. Hello, I'm Jackson Purdy.

LUCINDA. My name's Lucinda Harris.

VICTOR. Lucinda, I love you!

HARRIET. Don't get too excited. He loves everybody.

VICTOR. I don't love Jackson.

JACKSON *(to LUCINDA)*. You're new, aren't you? Did you bring your camera?

LUCINDA. Well, sure, I always bring my camera when I…

JACKSON. Wonderful. We've been waiting all day. We don't have much time. We'll lose the light. *(Beginning to arrange people for a group picture.)* Amy Lynn...stand over here by the lemonade stand. Victor, stand behind something and...

VICTOR. Stand behind something!

AMY LYNN. Jackson, I don't want to have my picture...

JACKSON. Maurice, would you mind standing over there by...*(JACKSON is picking up papers, odds and ends to make the site more attractive.)*

LUCINDA *(overlapping).* I think there may be a mistake.

HARRIET. Jackson, you've...

MAURICE. I'm fine where I am, Jackson.

VICTOR. Everybody's fine, Jackson 'cept you! Don't you get it?

COLLEEN *(to LUCINDA).* Where are you from?

LUCINDA. Every summer I pick a...

JACKSON. The *Times Record* must be expanding their staff. That's a good sign. Means the county's growin'. Told ya! Harold, stand over here and...

HAROLD. Don't you push me around, you foreigner.

AMY LYNN. We should leave now, Jackson. This doesn't feel right.

STANLEY *(to LUCINDA).* I have my notes here if you want to see them.

JACKSON *(to LUCINDA).* Is Channel 9 on their way, do you know?

COLLEEN. I don't think she's in television, Jackson.

LUCINDA. I hitchhike. Ride the bus sometimes. I meet a lot of people that way.

JACKSON *(beat).* You're not the photographer from the *Times Record?*

LUCINDA. No.

JACKSON. Where's the photographer from the *Times Record*?

LUCINDA. I don't know. The bus driver let me off by the Dairy Queen. Didn't look open, though.

JACKSON *(with a slightly frantic intensity)*. It'll be open in a jiffy soon as we all get off our butts and click this town into high gear.

VICTOR. That's a hell of a speech, Jackson. I think you're on your way!

AMY LYNN *(to LUCINDA)*. Are you thirsty?

LUCINDA. Not really.

AMY LYNN. I've got a little lemonade left and I have some...

LUCINDA. That's okay. I've got to be going.

AMY LYNN *(with desperation)*. Please stay! Don't leave! I have some chicken that I fixed and no one's eaten any!

STANLEY. It's very good, Amy Lynn, but I'm not...

AMY LYNN. Please!

MAURICE. It's the heat, Amy Lynn. It kills the appetite.

GEORGIA. I've always liked how you make it so moist.

JACKSON *(angrily)*. Jesus! We aren't trading recipes here! We're trying to get to the doorstep of the future...

AMY LYNN. Don't you talk to me in that tone of voice again, Jackson. I'll leave with Colleen.

JACKSON. We've got to push back the envelope, get with the program. *(Begins to pick up random items around the tree.)* Help me clean up this mess.

AMY LYNN. I'm just trying to be hospitable. You hear me? Colleen, can I come along with you?

HARRIET. This is our rumpus room, Jackson. Leave it alone.

AMY LYNN *(to JACKSON)*. I can't take any more.

JACKSON. Not now, Amy Lynn.

AMY LYNN *(with focus and energy).* Yes, now! There's never a good time. Whenever I want to talk you're at a meeting or on the phone. All I see is you running out the door. And I stay behind to fry the chicken, or get the bake sale organized. I'm not even a good cook, Jackson. Stanley's just being polite. He can barely keep it down. The lemonade's not sweet enough. No one laughs at your jokes. You try too hard. We've got to stop running. *(JACKSON stops and looks at AMY LYNN. He senses her tension.)* She died, sweetheart. That doesn't make us bad people. She wasn't even born yet but she died. We don't have to go around begging to be accepted! We didn't do anything wrong. *(To ALL.)* Did we? Did we do anything wrong?

JACKSON. Amy Lynn. Honey...let's get you back to the house for a rest...

AMY LYNN *(to ALL).* Well, did we? I want to know. Please. If we're going to get up tomorrow morning...and the next day and the next day after that and do this all over again, I have to know it's the right thing to...

JACKSON. I'm sorry, everyone. She's not herself since...

HARRIET. Don't apologize for your wife, Jackson. Don't you hear her?

HAROLD. You're embarrassed by her, aren't you? That's no way to make a marriage, young man. This is a major moment here.

JACKSON *(to ALL).* We don't know you! She shouldn't talk like this in front of you. She's tired is all.

HAROLD. You don't give us a chance to know you. Want to bring a super highway through the middle of Four Way... cut down our forest here...and make us sleep in the Ramada Inn. Would you like to know a person like that? Well? Would you?

JACKSON (*exhausted, drops the items he's been gathering*). I was trying to do something here. (*Beat.*) Make something grow.

MAURICE. You have a chance to make something grow now.

GEORGIA. Right here. This very moment.

COLLEEN. Tell her you love her, Jackson. That's where it all starts. And mean it. A woman knows when you don't mean it.

GEORGIA. We can take a lot if you love us.

HAROLD. Listen to that old lady. She speaks the truth.

JACKSON. This is none of your affair. This is private.

COLLEEN. Nothing in this town is private, Jackson.

HARRIET. We're all the same person. It all goes a lot easier if you accept that.

VICTOR. Got to tell 'em you love 'em…at least once a year…or they forget. Isn't that right, Harriet?

HARRIET. Keeps us comin' back for more.

COLLEEN. I'll take once a year.

HAROLD. They do some strange things now and then.

GEORGIA. Harold, behave yourself.

BOBBY JAMES. This is stupid.

CHERYL MAE. Hush up and listen.

VICTOR. You watch how big people deal with problems, kid, or I'll break your other arm.

GEORGIA. She wants to hear it, Jackson. (*The tension builds. ALL are looking at JACKSON.*)

VICTOR. Hell, we all want to hear it! (*JACKSON quickly exits the stage.*)

HARRIET (*to VICTOR*). Your timing stinks.

GEORGIA. Some men are like that, Amy Lynn. Emotion scares them.

BOBBY JAMES. Is that how you solve your problems? Run away? Thanks for the lesson.

HAROLD. It ain't over 'til the fat lady sings. Remember that.

AMY LYNN. It's all right. The doctor said I might have some problems if I got pregnant...but we wanted a child. Both of us. Maybe even Jackson more than me. He had driven over to Stallingsburg for the Rotary luncheon... make some contacts and do the right thing. Then he stayed longer to talk to a banker about loaning us the money to add on an extra room for the baby and when he came home...I'd been on the floor for a while...he put me in the car...and drove me to the hospital in Ralston. He thinks he's to blame. *(Beat.)* We thought things would be different here. But he had to keep on going so he went to more meetings. Even when there weren't any meetings...he called them just so he'd have something to build on, he said. A foundation.

(DARYL enters dressed in jeans and a short sleeved shirt. He's cleaned up and has combed his hair. He's carrying the "time capsule.")

DARYL. Mr. Purdy's sitting in the hole in the middle of the street. Looks like he's been crying. Is he all right?

AMY LYNN. He's probably just resting. That's all. It's been a hard day for him. Things haven't gone too well. I'll go see if...*(Exits.)*

DARYL *(to CHERYL MAE)*. Hi.

CHERYL MAE. Hi.

DARYL. You look nice.

CHERYL MAE. Thanks. So do you.

DARYL. I brought this box back. Mr. Purdy put it in the back of the truck while we were digging up some of the rocks.

STANLEY. History.

DARYL. Sir?

STANLEY. That was history you were digging up.

DARYL. I'm sorry. I didn't mean to destroy something important.

CHERYL MAE. It's not your fault.

GEORGIA *(to LUCINDA)*. The first settler in Four Way.

LUCINDA. Oh.

GEORGIA *(to LUCINDA)*. It's our birthday. We're one hundred and sixty-seven years old today.

MAURICE. Where it all began. He stuck it out through thick and thin. Musta been lonely. Others came along in time and stayed. That's how it all happens. Takes time.

HARRIET. Takes a lot of courage.

STANLEY. Can't just pave it over. We'll forget who we are.

VICTOR. I'm forgetting that right now.

HAROLD. Does that mean the game's over? We missed the 21st Century? *(In a surprisingly frantic manner.)* Computers doing stuff to us...gettin' into our lives...into our bank accounts...telephone calls...give 'em your zip code and they can tell how tall ya are and how many ties ya got in your closet...

GEORGIA. Harold, are you all right?

HARRIET *(to LUCINDA)*. The heat gets ya. Kinda like malaria.

HAROLD. Doctors' records...who ya voted for...

COLLEEN. Can't do anything but wait it out.

HAROLD. What ya have for breakfast...

HARRIET. Need some rain bad.

HAROLD. And lunch and dinner.

GEORGIA. That's why I bring my umbrella. Bring us some luck. And Maurice brings his umbrella too, don't you, Maurice?

MAURICE. Every day for the last two months.

HAROLD. And what ya dream about!

BOBBY JAMES. I think Mr. Sweeney's lost it!

HAROLD. And even which position you enjoyed the most!

GEORGIA. Harold!

(JACKSON re-enters the scene carrying an ax. AMY LYNN enters with him.)

CHERYL MAE. Mr. Darcy?

GEORGIA. Oh, dear.

MAURICE. Jackson, why don't you put that down.

JACKSON. No.

VICTOR *(rising to his feet like John Wayne)*. Can't let you do this, pardner.

HARRIET. We've got it all now. Paul Bunyan vs. John Wayne.

BOBBY JAMES. This is cool. Something's finally gonna happen around here.

MAURICE. Why don't you think about this just a bit longer, Jackson?

JACKSON. I'm finished doing all the thinking I'm ever going to do about anything.

MAURICE. This isn't a wise decision.

JACKSON. Something's got to happen for me. Now. Right now.

AMY LYNN. Jackson, you're frightening me.

JACKSON. I want to start over, Amy Lynn. Level. Everything even. Build it up right.

AMY LYNN. Please, sweetheart.

VICTOR *(advancing toward JACKSON)*. Put it down, Jackson.

JACKSON. Stay where you are, Victor.

HAROLD. Cuttin' this tree is like cutting ourselves.

MAURICE. We'll all bleed, Jackson.

VICTOR. Done enough bleedin' in my life time.

GEORGIA. Where would we come to visit each other? Find out whether Bobby James is going to get that new pick-up he's been working for.

BOBBY JAMES. Damn bank says I don't have enough...

CHERYL MAE. That's just an example, Bobby James.

STANLEY (*as if possessed by a growing inner strength*). Its branches...spreading...to protect us from the searing pain of the world! Who will protect us when it's gone? (*Opening his arms wide to create a barrier between JACKSON and the tree. A long silence.*)

JACKSON (*beat*). Nothing I do is ever finished. Something always happens. The photographer never came. The cameras never came. Pizza Surprise...Pizza Hut...Shoney's... Ramada Inn...Holiday Inn...Quality Inn...Budget Inn... they're all out. No one ever called me back. No one knows I'm alive. No one knows I'm here.

LUCINDA. I know you're here. That's why I came. Saw the balloons down by the highway. "Happy Birthday Four Way. 167 Years of Happiness and Sunshine." Saw the sign and told the bus driver to drop me off...that I was interested in seeing 167 years of happiness and sunshine.

HARRIET. Well, it's a bit cloudy right now, but we'll brighten it up for ya in a minute or two.

JACKSON. I didn't put out any balloons down by the turn off.

AMY LYNN (*beat*). I did.

JACKSON. When?

AMY LYNN. After our fight.

JACKSON. It wasn't a fight. It was a discussion.

AMY LYNN. I yelled and you yelled.

JACKSON (*exhaustion gets the better of him. He lowers the ax*). I just wanted you to come to bed.

AMY LYNN. There was so much to finish.

JACKSON. You're working too hard.

AMY LYNN. I had things to get ready for the garage sale.

JACKSON. I said I'd help you in the morning.

AMY LYNN. I don't know what to feel if I'm not busy! If I stop working, then I'll have to think and I'm afraid of what I'll think...and feel...and do. I knew today was important to you. I drove down to the turn off and blew up those balloons and got the magic markers and made the sign. It got a little crooked. One of the headlights burned out. Then I came back. Put the toasters and the plates by the door so I'd remember to take them this morning. And the crock pot you dropped two years ago and the three ties Mother bought you last Christmas...

JACKSON. I promised you I'd wear them.

AMY LYNN. ...and turned out the light and came to bed.

JACKSON. I watched from the kitchen until I couldn't see the tail lights anymore. I thought you were leaving me. Then I sat on the back deck just looking up at the sky. It was awful being there by myself. All I wanted to do was get close to you so you'd never leave me. Then you came back and I didn't know what to say so I went inside and crawled back into bed.

AMY LYNN. You didn't move.

JACKSON. I thought if I moved...you'd leave me again. *(Beat.)* I...Amy Lynn? Oh, Jesus.

VICTOR *(beat)*. You almost did it there, Jackson.

HARRIET. Victor!

VICTOR. You gonna do it now? You gonna tell her you love her? We're all waitin'.

BOBBY JAMES. Yeah, I wish you would. I gotta take a... *(HAROLD says "Hush" to BOBBY JAMES as ALL look at JACKSON.)*

JACKSON (*as if a fever has just been broken*). I love you, Amy Lynn.

HAROLD. Did he say it?

GEORGIA. Oh, Harold.

HAROLD. I couldn't hear him. I don't hear so well, ya know.

VICTOR. We have to shoot another take, Jackson. The sound man was out to lunch.

JACKSON. I love you. Don't leave me.

AMY LYNN. I love you, too.

GEORGIA (*to HAROLD*). She said she loved him, too.

HAROLD. I heard her. It's him I didn't hear.

BOBBY JAMES. This is mushy. I got to go take a...

CHERYL MAE. Bobby James!

BOBBY JAMES. Nobody lets me finish a sentence around here!

JACKSON (*to AMY LYNN*). I want you to be proud of me. I don't want you to be sorry you ever married me. I don't want to be a...failure. And after our baby died...

AMY LYNN. It wasn't your fault...and you're not a failure, sweetheart. We just have to rest a bit. We can't keep going like this. (*Takes JACKSON into her arms.*)

HAROLD. Take time to smell the tulips.

GEORGIA. There are no tulips in Four Way, Harold.

HAROLD. It's an expression, Georgia. I'm just trying to make a contribution here.

GEORGIA. I've been hauling you around for decades.

HAROLD. Now don't you start on me, Georgia.

GEORGIA. When was the last time you said you loved me? You can't remember, can you?

VICTOR. Oh, oh.

HAROLD. Georgia, everybody's looking.

HARRIET (*to MAURICE*). Did you tell Margaret you loved her, Maurice?

MAURICE. Yes.

HAROLD. Every day?

MAURICE. Not as often as I think she wanted to hear it…nor as often as I really wanted to say it.

HAROLD. Did she know?

MAURICE. I hope so.

HAROLD *(to GEORGIA)*. Of course I love you, Georgia. Wouldn't have spent forty eight years of my life with you if I didn't.

VICTOR. That's not a slam dunk, Harold. Gotta do it all the way.

HAROLD. Oh…*(Beat.)*…I…love…you.

VICTOR. I didn't hear that. Did the rest of you hear that?

COLLEEN *(to CHERYL MAE and DARYL)*. Hope you're learning how to be adults by watching all these big people.

DARYL. They're just like my grandparents.

HAROLD *(yelling)*. I love you! There! Everybody hear that!

GEORGIA. I hear you, Harold. That's so sweet of you.

VICTOR. I love you, Harriet. Ever tell you that?

HARRIET. Every year, Victor. Set my watch by it.

VICTOR *(jumping up into the air)*. Hell, I think I love everybody! *(He begins to move in a free form dance-like manner.)*

HARRIET. Victor, it's supper time. We're all done here for the day, so let's pack it in.

VICTOR. Don't ya feel it? It's in the air.

HARRIET. Nothin' in the air but the heat, honey. Let's go now.

VICTOR. It's gonna rain!

STANLEY. Hasn't rained in fifty-three days. I've been keeping a record right here…somewhere.

VICTOR *(to BOBBY JAMES)*. Make me some sounds, boy. I feel the spirit! *(BOBBY JAMES begins to beat out a rhyth-

mical underscore to VICTOR's rising fervor.) Yeah, good. Keep it up!

BOBBY JAMES. Ho, ho!

HARRIET. Victor, tomorrow we're driving you to the V.A. hospital! *(VICTOR sweeps HARRIET into his arms.)* Let me go. Now.

VICTOR. Let yourself go! Feel the spirit. Let the truth wash you clean.

HARRIET. The truth is…you need help.

VICTOR. Be my woman, Harriet. Come to me…and never let me go!

BOBBY JAMES. I don't believe this!

COLLEEN. Let the truth wash you clean…oh, yeah! Do it, Harriet. It feels good. *(COLLEEN begins to move also, but her movements are more seductive… not lewd but clearly suggestive of a sensual awareness. BOBBY JAMES picks up the tempo a bit.)*

HAROLD. Look at her, will ya?

GEORGIA. Have some lemonade, Harold.

VICTOR *(to MAURICE).* Is it raining yet, Maurice?

MAURICE *(smiling).* Any minute now, Victor.

AMY LYNN *(beginning to move.)* Jackson, you want to dance?

JACKSON. Aren't we tired? I thought we were tired?

COLLEEN. She doesn't look tired to me, Jackson.

AMY LYNN. Come on, sweetheart. Just move side to side.

JACKSON *(beginning to move to the beat. He is shy but slowly begins to find the rhythm).* The reporter from the *Times Record* could come along any minute.

VICTOR. No one's coming, Jackson. We're the town that time forgot.

HAROLD. I saw that movie. Big lizards ate everybody up.

GEORGIA (*rising to her feet and beginning to dance*). This feels good, Harold. Try it. Come on.

HAROLD. It looks painful to me.

GEORGIA (*opening up her arms*). Come to me, darling. Come on.

JACKSON. I feel silly. Can we leave now?

VICTOR. Hold her in your arms, Jackson. She's your salvation. She's gonna kill herself cooking pies for bake sales 'less you save her.

GEORGIA. Free. Free. Free! This is wonderful.

(JACKSON sheepishly takes AMY LYNN into his arms.

HAROLD, unable finally to remain seated any longer, rises to his feet as well and begins to dance with GEORGIA.

DARYL looks at CHERYL MAE who shakes her head "no." He begins to dance by himself. His movements are more clearly shaped. He may, actually, be doing a rain dance. After several moments CHERYL MAE joins him.

Even MAURICE begins to move. Dignified, graceful.

LUCINDA begins to sing a song...perhaps a church hymn, a folk song. Or maybe she just harmonizes with whatever sounds and rhythms BOBBY JAMES is making.

COLLEEN goes to STANLEY who is transfixed by all that he sees. She extends her hand to him. They dance.

The dance movements should remind us of a time when all inhabitants of the village came together to pray to the gods for sustenance and salvation.

At the height of the dancing there is a loud and dominant thunder clap. Not everyone hears it. Thunder sounds again. This time the thunder is heard and ALL except DARYL stop dancing. After a moment DARYL stops his dancing.)

VICTOR. Well, what do you say to that, eh?

HAROLD. That's heat lighting, that's all.

COLLEEN. Are you sure?

AMY LYNN. Are those clouds over there? Look. *(Several look out.)*

HAROLD. Yeah. See 'em?

STANLEY. I think Victor's right.

COLLEEN *(to LUCINDA)*. You have a lovely voice.

LUCINDA. Thank you. I got it from my mother.

BOBBY JAMES. I did pretty good, didn't I?

VICTOR. You got great potential, kid.

BOBBY JAMES. Yeah. Think I'll be a drummer. Yeah. Whew. Hot. That was neat.

HARRIET. Well, when you let it all hang out, it kinda goes everywhere. That's it for me. Come on, Victor. Day's over. *(ALL begin gathering up their items and "coming down" from the euphoria of the dance experience. HARRIET goes to the laundry pile and selects an old towel or two to pass around. The color of the sky is beginning to turn. All of these changes blend into and around the new mood which has emerged... the new feeling of acceptance....)*

MAURICE *(to COLLEEN)*. Anything I can do, Colleen?

COLLEEN. Nope! Cold turkey. Time to go.

MAURICE. You'll call?

COLLEEN. I will. Yeah. Let me get settled in...whatever that means. Am I doing the right thing, Maurice?

CHERYL MAE *(to DARYL)*. Was that a real Indian dance?

DARYL. My grandfather taught me a few steps. When I was eight I would watch him at sunset. Looked like he was dancin' in the center of the sun. You still want to go out for pizza?

CHERYL MAE. I have to take Bobby James back to the...

MAURICE. I'll drive Bobby James back to the house, Cheryl Mae.

STANLEY *(stepping forward)*. I want to. I want to drive. Bobby James?

BOBBY JAMES. What?

STANLEY. I'll take you back home when it's time. If that's okay with you.

BOBBY JAMES *(beat)*. I gotta stop in at the Oasis...play some videos.

STANLEY. I'll wait. *(HAROLD and GEORGIA gather up their materials.)*

GEORGIA. Well, thank you everybody for an interesting day. Happy Birthday.

JACKSON. Nobody came.

VICTOR. Hell, we're here. What more do you need?

HARRIET. Anybody who's anybody is here. That's what really matters.

GEORGIA. Aren't you somebody, Harold?

HAROLD. What?

GEORGIA. Of course you are, sweetheart.

HAROLD. Of course I am what? Keep it simple, woman.

JACKSON. No front page picture. Stanley, do you have any Polaroids left...something...anything?

STANLEY. I'm all out.

LUCINDA. I have some film. I'll take your picture.

JACKSON. What's that?

LUCINDA. I always take pictures. Put them on my computer. I'm a computer programmer. Watch the screen all day you think your whole world is inside a little box. Have to get out. Meet people. Or you forget you're human. Begin to think like a machine. Pictures tell me who I am.

JACKSON. You will?

LUCINDA. Sure, why not?

VICTOR. Great idea. Yo! Everyone! It's picture time. Front and center. I love having my picture taken.

JACKSON (to LUCINDA). That's very nice of...are you going to charge anything?

AMY LYNN. Jackson.

JACKSON. Sorry. All right. Colleen and Cheryl Mae...you stand over here and Harriet, you move in behind...(He notices that no one is moving.) Oh, what difference does it make! Stand wherever you want. (ALL adjust themselves around the tree, on the tree bench and on the ground. Ad libs should carry the moment. "Over here by me, Harold." "Does anybody have a comb?" "Last picture I had taken was in the 10th grade." "This is really stupid." "I want copies." "Tuck your shirt in." BOBBY JAMES goes to the fireworks and pulls out several sparklers. "Here, light these!" He hands them to VICTOR, STANLEY and a few others. The final arrangement should have the look of a 4th of July picnic photo.)

GEORGIA. This is better than a time capsule, isn't it, Harold?

HAROLD. This is a time capsule, Georgia.

LUCINDA (has taken her position in front of the group). Heads up everyone. Ready?

VICTOR (yelling). Geronimo! (Several people are startled.)

MAURICE. I think the operative word is cheese, Victor.

LUCINDA. Everyone? One...two...three...(*Everyone says "cheese". She takes the picture just as lightning flashes. The effect, combined with the changing light of the sunset, reminds us of a sepia toned "old time" photograph. For a moment the effect is frozen in time.*)

JACKSON (*beat*). Did you get it?

LUCINDA. Got it.

GEORGIA. That was nice.

JACKSON (*to LUCINDA*). Thank you.

LUCINDA. Sure. This is the best birthday party I've been to in years. (*No one moves. It is as if there is a sense of solidarity that is felt by everyone. There is a quiet laugh or two, almost a nervous giggle. After a moment, the composition begins to dissolve.*)

AMY LYNN. I have to fix dinner, Jackson. It's getting late.

JACKSON. I'm coming. (*To LUCINDA.*) Can I have the film so I can develop it in the morning?

LUCINDA. I'll send you the negative when I finish the roll.

JACKSON. I'd really rather...you will?

LUCINDA. I promise.

JACKSON. That'll be fine. Thank you.

BOBBY JAMES. Come on, Stanley. Meet ya at the Oasis. I'll beat your ass all over the place. (*BOBBY JAMES picks up a few more of the fireworks and exits.*) Boy, what a dumb day!

CHERYL MAE. Bobby James, I see you!

COLLEEN (*to LUCINDA*). Do you want a lift? Those two hat boxes gave me an empty passenger seat. Come along as far as you like.

LUCINDA. Where are you going?

COLLEEN. I'm not sure.

LUCINDA. Yeah. I do. Thanks. I'll ride with you.

JACKSON. You can send the picture to...

COLLEEN. Learn to bake a cake, Jackson. I'll take care of the picture. Cheryl Mae...I'll call...we can talk...tell me how pretty you look. Remember what I said. Stanley, thanks for the dance. Bye, everybody. Damn! *(COLLEEN and LUCINDA exit.)*

VICTOR. No hoops tonight, eh, Cheryl Mae?

CHERYL MAE. Tomorrow, okay?

VICTOR. Yeah, tomorrow's fine.

GEORGIA. You say hello to your aunt for me, young man.

DARYL. Yes, ma'am. I will. Mr. Purdy? I called the department again. And we'll have to cement over the rocks and things we found if we're gonna put in a stop sign. And they said we couldn't put the box under the sign. They called it a wrinkle in the system. They aren't real big on wrinkles. They want you to call 'em in the morning and talk about it.

STANLEY. We can't cement it over. Can't lock away our history.

VICTOR. Can't cut down the tree, either. What to do...what to do!

HARRIET. Well, Jackson?

JACKSON. Tomorrow. We'll get together at the Oasis. All of us can talk about what we should do. Then we'll decide.

HAROLD. And none of those outsiders. Just the town. Us. We should be making our own decisions.

GEORGIA. You old activist, you.

HAROLD. Maybe we'll vote to do nothing...just live the best we can.

VICTOR. Maybe even vote to keep out the 21st Century.

MAURICE. We can't do that, Victor. It's coming at us over the hill.

STANLEY. I want to keep the minutes.

VICTOR. Who's buyin' the donuts?

JACKSON. Dutch treat.

VICTOR. It's a deal.

HAROLD. Deal! Victor, I'm not finished with you yet!

VICTOR. I won't touch a card, Harold. It'll be here in the morning.

HAROLD *(to MAURICE)*. Then you'll be next on my list, Maurice.

MAURICE. I look forward to it, Harold. *(JACKSON and AMY LYNN are loaded up. JACKSON begins pushing off the lemonade stand.)*

GEORGIA. Wonderful chicken, Amy Lynn.

AMY LYNN. That's thoughtful of you, Georgia.

GEORGIA. Harold.

HAROLD. What?

GEORGIA. Lemonade!

HAROLD. Loved your lemonade, Amy Lynn. *(To GEORGIA.)* It wasn't that good. *(HAROLD and GEORGIA exit in the opposite direction.)*

MAURICE. Good night, Jackson.

JACKSON. Good night...everyone. *(JACKSON and AMY LYNN exit.)*

DARYL. You ready, Cheryl Mae?

CHERYL MAE *(to ALL)*. Good night, everybody.

DARYL. It was nice meeting all of you. Happy birthday. I'll be over again when you figure out what to do about the stop sign. *(DARYL and CHERYL MAE exit.)*

VICTOR *(helping HARRIET pick up the garage sale items)*. So, what now? We've got the past behind us and the future ahead of us. Hell of a mess. Tomorrow's my last day, Harriet. I've had it, you hear me!

HARRIET. I always hear ya, Victor. *(HARRIET and VICTOR begin to exit.)*

VICTOR. I miss Jimmy Loon. Miss him everyday.

HARRIET. I know you do, sweetheart. Maurice, say good night to Margaret for me. *(HARRIET and VICTOR exit.)*

STANLEY. I've got to go, Maurice. Don't want Bobby James to think I can't take a beating. There's so much to living, isn't there? See you tomorrow. *(Exits.)*

MAURICE *(is attentive, as if feeling someone's presence. He gathers up his items).* We're something, aren't we, Margaret? Try to force things to happen and nothing seems to go right. Don't try too hard and miracles occur. Good night, sweetheart. *(Beat.)* I miss your voice. *(Turns, begins to exit. Telephone rings. Thunder is heard close by. MAURICE pauses, looks up at the sky and smiles. He "throws a kiss to Margaret." The telephone stops ringing. He opens his umbrella and exits as the lights slowly fade to black.)*

CURTAIN

END OF PLAY

ADDITIONAL CHARACTER NOTES

MAURICE DARCY: Well dressed, wears spats. Congenial, well spoken, forgiving.

CHERYL MAE DOBBINS: An athlete with feminine grace.

"VULGAR" VICTOR BOSCO: His behavior is often unpredictable but never harmful.

STANLEY FRANK: Nervous, seldom completes a sentence, shy.

COLLEEN KIMBEL: Six months pregnant. Attractive, mysterious.

HARRIET MUELLER: Blunt but sensitive. A former Army nurse who has seen it all, she runs a small store and cares for "Vulgar" Victor.

JACKSON PURDY: A city-bred man who has become the self-appointed head of Four Way's one-man Chamber of Commerce. Hasn't yet discovered the town's rhythms.

BOBBY JAMES DOBBINS: Moody, naive, seeks attention.

AMY LYNN PURDY: High-strung, tries to please. Recently lost her first child to a miscarriage.

GEORGIA SWEENEY: Gracious, polite, former school teacher. Has difficulty seeing.

HAROLD SWEENEY: Crusty, complaining. Former sales manager, has difficulty hearing.

DARYL SWEETWOOD: Of Native American heritage. Pleasant demeanor.

DIRECTOR'S NOTES

DIRECTOR'S NOTES

DIRECTOR'S NOTES